The Magic of Fishing

John Moorwood

GREAT NORTHERN

Great Northern Books
PO Box 1380, Bradford,
West Yorkshire, BD5 5FB

www.greatnorthernbooks.co.uk

ISBN: 978-1-914227-13-4

Cover design and illustration
by Anna Stephenson

Illustrations by Rowan Moorwood

CIP Data
A catalogue for this book is available
from the British Library

This book is dedicated to
Joe and Iris, Rowan and Janet,
my fantastic family
and all of my fishing friends,
past and present.

CONTENTS

FOREWORD

By Dominic Garnett

If there are more words than ever written about angling, it's rather a shame that so few transcend the scope of "how to" articles, social media posts or unabashed marketing. There's nothing wrong with these straightforward means of messaging; but the more hurried the world becomes, the more I crave deeper, better quality storytelling.

This is why it has been a delightful surprise to delve into the manuscript you now have in your hands. By his own admission, the author has never fished for England, been courted by tackle giants or broken any major records. Yet perhaps this is precisely why *The Magic of Fishing* is such an enjoyable and relatable journey?

Encouragingly, I am sent various articles and stories by aspiring wordsmiths every season. Even those a little rough around the edges are great fun, and I enjoy reading them and offering what advice I can. Just occasionally, however, something a little bit special hits my inbox. The chapters of this very book have been some of the best I've had the pleasure of reading in a long while. A timely reminder, perhaps, of the power of the "ordinary" angler to spell out just how precious fishing is and take us back to its fundamentals.

I'm not talking about essentials like tying knots or killer rigs here, but the emotions and experiences that captivate each of us in a way that is both universal yet intensely personal. Like the relationships forged and indelible memories made over years of adventure. The smell of homemade bait, the cool of the dawn, or that "potent cocktail of hope, excitement and a touch of superstition" that precedes the first cast on any new water, as John puts it. I really couldn't have put it better myself.

I've read few better accounts of the breathless excitement of childhood fishing, come to think of it, let alone the evolution an angler goes through across decades, venues and experiences. I'd include many of angling's big hitters here, who might have enviable lists of accomplishments but nothing like the same ability to get below the surface of angling and connect with the rest of us.

Indeed, like John, I too remember a small farm pond with bottomless mystery. I, too, owned the *KnowHow Book of Fishing* and was hoodwinked by its boundless optimism and crap floats made out of ping-pong balls and drinking straws. And I, too, reached a point where angling became not just a hobby but deliverance from complete meltdown.

I say "ordinary" angler with caution, too, because the author has had a rich and varied life in fishing. From a tiny pool a few miles outside Sheffield, to trout streams, match fishing events and journeys to my home county of Devon and even The Gambia, this is a book that just about any keen all-round angler will enjoy.

However, it's perhaps the characters that really set *The Magic of Fishing* apart, along with a certain tenderness and attention to the small yet significant details that colour any keen angler's life. The author's original fishing mentor, his grandfather, is drawn with a particular poignancy. You can virtually smell his pipe and homemade bread paste!

Besides waters explored and fish landed, then, there is truth, love and loss in these pages. Indeed, as we emerge from the fear and drudgery of Covid, the themes of mental health, mortality and companionship have never been more pressing. Nor has the need to celebrate the finer and subtler qualities of this truly magical pastime of ours.

PREFACE

I always wanted to write a book about fishing, yet even in my 43rd year, and with a one-off career break at my disposal, I continued to resist the urge to celebrate my lifelong passion in prose. Despite a dawning realisation that I finally had some spare time on my hands, there always seemed to be other priorities, like sleeping.

There were plenty of other excuses too, the first and most obvious being that I've never caught a record-breaking fish or indeed anything particularly remarkable – at least not compared to the jaw-dropping specimens that regularly appear in the angling press. I like to think that's because I've not dedicated the majority of my time to pursuing scaly monsters, which is also a convenient excuse for not having attained Zen-like skills worthy of a YouTube channel.

In fact, I'm just another fisherman, one of the hordes of angling-obsessed people who spend most of their lives working or with their families, but sometimes find an opportunity to visit a lake, river or canal and lose themselves in another world for a few hours. Therefore, what right did I have to describe my bankside exploits and expect others to want to read about them? None, I told myself once again.

However, the second reason for this particular bout of writer's block was even more crippling. During the first glorious weeks of garden leave from a previous job, in between polishing up my CV and attending coffee meetings in London, I lay outside in the July heat and re-read my collection of books by Chris Yates.

For the uninitiated, I'm talking about Chris Yates, the author, naturalist and photographer; Chris Yates, the captor of the one-time biggest carp in Britain; and Chris Yates, the traditional and mildly eccentric angler, famed for his use of antique tackle, the simplest of tactics and a lifetime of watercraft to outwit his quarry.

He is also a dazzling writer and while there are many exceptional publications on the subject of fishing his are perhaps my favourite. As I read them again that summer, I was transported far from my garden in Surrey and taken back in time by tales so vivid I could almost smell the early morning vapours rising from the weir pools and estate lakes he described.

Yet for all the enjoyment the books gave me, I was left feeling my literary limitations more keenly. I was at once inspired and daunted, as his words touched on some of my own cherished memories while also seeming to come from another universe. I soaked up stories about the wondrous captures and many famous venues he's haunted over the decades, knowing I could never hope to emulate them, and even began to wonder if I'd misspent my prime years, as Mr Yates is a man who *has* managed to dedicate much of his life to piscatorial matters.

So, with all these doubts and so little time, why are these words suddenly appearing on a screen now that the garden is gripped by frost? Why am I typing, almost in a fever, and daring to dream that a publisher or unknown reader might one day find some merit in my own angling tales? It's quite simple really: over those few precious months of relative leisure time, I also rediscovered the magic of fishing.

I'd never really lost touch with it completely, but my reawakening began when I decided to emulate Chris's simple approach and get back to basics myself – enjoying it so much that I ended up spending more hours by the water than I'd managed for many years. And during that glut of time in the countryside, often alone and always far from busy offices and endless emails, I again felt the childlike pleasure of trying to catch whatever might swim in front of me.

I was recharged with an incurable excitement first kindled beside a tiny farm pond in Derbyshire, while also recalling the many adventures my hobby had gone on to provide as I grew up in Sheffield. Over more recent years, that thrill never quite died, but it had been stifled by 21st-century life and its myriad stresses. As if shaking off a lingering illness, I gradually remembered what had first captured my imagination and, by the time winter blasted its first icy breaths over the countryside, I knew for sure it's the magical element of fishing that really counts.

'Magic' is one of the few words that does justice to the sheer joy of one of Earth's most popular and ancient pastimes. It's also a common strand of many great stories of course and, on this aspect of fishing at least, I suddenly realised that I had plenty to impart.

I'm talking about the kind of magic felt by a five-year-old waking up on Christmas morning, nervously checking to see if the empty stocking hung on the end of their bed is somehow bulky with presents. It's a fluttery, giddy and overwhelmingly happy sensation that can materialise when treading down a familiar path towards a secluded pool, or during a restless night spent planning an exploratory trip to a new venue.

Many British anglers feel it most intensely on the 15th of June, the evening before the new season begins on our rivers, but it can touch those who are afflicted all year round and no matter where they live. Best of all, anyone who fishes can experience it, and you don't need to shatter records, have access to exclusive fisheries or be able to name-drop angling royalty.

Nor do you need expensive tackle, realms of experience or detailed instruction manuals. I know this to be true because I'm lucky enough to have felt it, and witness it in others, over many years. So, if you have too, or even if you're perplexed but open-minded about the existence of magic, then read on.

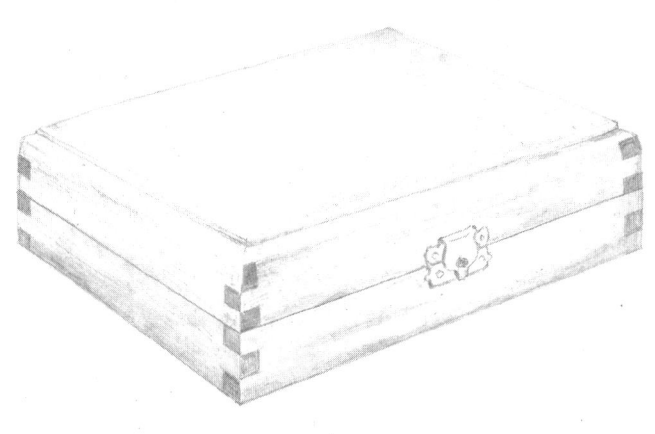

CHAPTER 1

A Box of Tricks

If it weren't for Joe Moorwood, a retired steelworker and my paternal granddad, I might never have joined fishing's magic circle. I was barely conscious of the world when he finally said goodbye to the volcanic furnaces and ceaseless din of the rolling mill – replacing them with the cool sanctuary of his local pub, a steamy greenhouse full of pungent tomato plants, and a regular flutter in the bookies – but it was perfect timing.

He couldn't boil an egg or make a decent slice of toast, and luckily for him he never had to, but he could do lots of other interesting things. He could name every plant in his garden and advise how to grow them, fix troublesome car engines or make pirate cutlasses from rolled-up newspapers. And he could tell fascinating tales about his childhood in Sheffield: like having to go without proper shoes for a while, or how his own granddad had run away from home in a bid to become a teenage jockey.

Indeed, it seemed his youth had been full of strange and sometimes morbid events, including the time he left for school early one morning and came across a dead man. Granddad said his throat had been cut, perhaps by a rival gang member, and described how the lifeless body had been left seated on the ground in plain sight.

The victim's head and shoulders were propped up against some park railings, while his stiff, outstretched legs formed a triangular barrier around a dark, sticky pool of congealing blood. I couldn't imagine witnessing such a gruesome scene, never mind continuing to my lessons afterwards, so I quickly surmised that Granddad's formative years must have been very different from mine.

He had a kind and intelligent face that seldom became animated but could still speak volumes. For instance, when he smiled, his lips rarely parted and his pipe often remained clenched in one corner of his mouth, yet a simultaneous wink could convey his delight in something, along with a lifetime of working-class wisdom.

Gold-rimmed glasses and silvery, bushy eyebrows framed his expressive, pale blue eyes and he always combed his thinning, snow-white hair straight back, holding every strand neatly in place with Brylcreem. Most of his crown was still visible, though, which was often tanned and freckled from the long hours spent weeding the garden or fishing by a pond, yet his forehead remained remarkably smooth and ageless right into his eighties.

Whatever he was doing, he usually wore a buttoned shirt and although a cardigan might make an occasional appearance in winter I never saw him in a woolly jumper or the kind of informal, round-necked T-shirts that dominated my own child-sized wardrobe. He usually combined his shirts with grey, Farah flannel trousers and, if he was within a hundred yards of home, a pair of battered leather slippers which banished any hint of formality.

He didn't talk about his working life much, although he once told me that he'd never missed a single day at his firm with illness or any other excuse in nearly five decades. I still believe it, although he also confided that he *always* stopped for a quick pint on the way home, never once swerving from the sacred routine, which seems a little more incredible. Being equally fond of Grandma I was less sure what to make of that claim, but if indeed he managed it without exception for nearly half a century, it must surely be applauded for dedication.

Having given up cigarettes around the time he ended his weekday steel and beer odyssey, he still liked to smoke a pipe whenever he was outside and, not knowing the health implications back then, I indirectly enjoyed the habit too. Regular puffs of his tobacco smoke swirled lazily towards me as he tended his roses and, as it became diluted with enough fresh air, the vanilla-tinged clouds conjured up thoughts of caramel.

Fairly soon after retiring he became seriously ill, and even at my tender age I remember thinking how unjust that seemed. He was meant to be relaxing now, but instead he was in and out of Weston Park Hospital every week and looking worn out whenever we saw him at home. At one stage he turned bright green thanks to chemicals the doctors pumped into him. Mum had to explain it didn't actually give him the powers of the Incredible Hulk, but it still seemed special to me.

He lived with Hodgkin's disease for a couple of arduous, worrying years and eventually overcame it, although his energy was undeniably depleted and he suffered regular bouts of sweating. He could no longer control his body temperature and I often observed him studying the racing pages of a newspaper while holding a plastic, battery-operated fan to his face. Especially during summertime, the general rule was a fan when inside and a pipe for outside.

His lengthy and varied treatment also left him with a thick scar snaking down the middle of his chest, which I sometimes spied as his unbuttoned shirt flapped about on a breezy beach or pier. The cause was apparently some terrible operation that I couldn't begin to comprehend, although Dad once told me the surgeons had used metal clamps to prise his ribcage apart, so knowing just that much I believed he must be invincible.

My mum's parents unfortunately died long before I was born, and although I became close to my Aunty May and several other relations who had helped raise Mum during her teenage years in Bolton, it's perhaps another reason why my paternal grandparents became such a significant part of my life.

Joe lived with Iris, my grandma, on Downing Road, which was only a 15-minute drive away from home. As a young lad I easily confused their address with London's Downing Street and for a number of years believed it to be even more special than it might have already been – wilfully ignoring the fact their home was actually a modest semi-detached house towards the top of one of the city's seven hills.

Our visits there were so regular and full of anticipation that I could shut my eyes during the journey and guess exactly where we were at any given point. And I knew the sight of their pebble-dashed house best of all, which confirmed we'd finally arrived. To its left was a small garage that Granddad had built himself, while in front there was just enough space to park their little touring caravan. Its cream walls blocked much of the daylight from their front room but provided years of memorable holidays to coastal retreats such as Scarborough and Whitby – so surely a worthwhile sacrifice.

Sandwiched between the house and garage was an ornate iron gate, which Grandma painstakingly coated with white gloss every other spring. And beyond that, down a short passageway paved with concrete slabs, was a wooden-framed, lean-to porch. We always passed by the 'official' front door, which was actually in the side of the house, and knocked on the thin glass panel of the porch door.

At this point I would hold my breath and jump about with excitement, as the brief clatter was guaranteed to bring Grandma rushing out to greet us in a whirlwind of mock surprise, genuine laughter and talcum-scented hugs. Only after we'd been sufficiently fussed over could I make my way into the porch, then through a flimsy sliding door into their miniscule kitchen and on into the back room with its familiar gas fire, brass ornaments and sheepskin rug.

Unless he was gardening, it was usually here that Granddad could be found – reading his paper, checking the racing results on Ceefax or slowly getting up from his comfy chair with a friendly smile. His greetings were modest compared to Grandma's, but no less warm or welcome.

He wasn't the only attraction inside the house, either. Soon after landing I would start looking for old cake tins in the kitchen, which were usually filled with freshly baked lemon curd tarts, coconut cake or flapjack. Or I'd hunt for half-hidden pots of boiled sweets, plastic tub-loads of old Dinky cars and tall bottles of fizzy drinks – 'pop' as Granddad called them – which were kept invitingly cool in a pantry under the stairs.

Not only were these resources hugely appealing to a young boy, but, initially at least, they felt like mine alone. My three younger siblings would eventually stake their claims too, but I was the eldest child and therefore the first with regular access. And being the eldest of four may also be one of the reasons Granddad adopted me as his only fishing apprentice – especially when combined with my boundless enthusiasm for sticklebacks and tadpoles.

I can't recall much from that embryonic phase of my fishing career, but I'm familiar with a faded, 1970s photograph of a toddler, sporting a shock of blonde curls and an earnest expression, peering over the concrete bank of a pond with a bamboo-handled fishing net in one fist. To be precise, it was taken at a local park pond called Forge Dam – a fertile cradle of life for many budding anglers in my neighbourhood.

Ultimately, however, my selection was probably down to the fact that only I seemed to *understand* the appeal of trying to catch fish. I don't wish to offend my brothers and sister – or indeed my dad, who didn't catch the bug despite his father's enthusiasm – but they never quite worked out what all the fuss was about. They have huge talents and interests in many other things, but I think fishing's something you either get or you don't and it's fair to say my family are in the majority.

I'm sure it's possible for non-believers to experience a spark of interest and it's not uncommon to draw gasps of astonishment or a flurry of questions from friendly passers-by who happen to witness a successful cast, but I've lost count of the hours I've spent trying to explain my fascination to others in any meaningful depth.

Whether it's a mate, colleague or recent acquaintance, it can feel like trying to remind a cynical, world-weary adult about the carefree wonder of early childhood.

People may comprehend the words coming out of my mouth, but their hearts remain unstirred and if someone can't *begin* to understand an obsession with fishing, it's difficult to convey any logic in the long hours spent doing it. Likewise, it's a tough sell on the endless gear one can accumulate, the bad weather sometimes endured, or, perhaps the ultimate taboo, the fact maggots keep best in the fridge.

I've therefore come to see the world a bit like JK Rowling because, where angling's concerned, I also think there are 'wizards' and 'muggles'. The term 'fishermuggles' might describe a large portion of the general public who find it impossible to comprehend the magnetic pull of a tranquil lake and its finned inhabitants.

Which isn't intended as a slur, but I think most people are oblivious to the almost-primal urge to touch these mysterious creatures, just for a moment, even when I clarify it's not to eat them – or not in my case, anyway. It's more about immersing myself in the natural world and playing a game with an incalculable number of variables. Not a cold, calculating game, but a fascinating, rewarding and life-affirming drive to engage with something unseen, unpredictable and unique.

Trying to explain my desire to understand, catch and admire fish usually leads to polite frowns, leg-pulling or utter bafflement. Indeed, the only people who seem to exist somewhere in between these two extremes of awareness are those related to, or in a relationship with, a fishing fanatic.

It seems that if a fishermuggle co-habits with someone who is under angling's spell for long enough they can gradually develop some tolerance of, or even a begrudging respect for, the afflicted. Nevertheless, a shared love of their offspring or partner's watery fixation is usually too much to hope for.

I'm willing to accept fishing is a somewhat strange pastime, and plenty of those who dedicate their lives to it might be described as eccentric too. I've met or still know many interesting, sociable and entertaining people who fish, and our ranks include plenty of popular celebrities and sporting stars, but it's not the coolest of hobbies.

Taking the mickey out of anglers is easy. For starters, I can't think of another hobby with more potential for innuendo. We're known to spend hours messing with our tackle, obsessing over rods, donning thigh-high rubber boots and choosing which waggler to use. If you want to include game fishing, of which I only have limited experience, there are buzzers to discuss, while sea anglers sometimes need to wear a butt-pad.

I can also appreciate that most people find pleasure in more 'normal' things, even if one of the joys of being on a riverbank is the break from normality it affords. I've met lots of adults who gave fishing a brief try as a youngster, usually with the encouragement of a keen but ultimately disappointed relation, but it's not generally something that busy people would consider dipping into, especially once they've found other things to take up their precious spare time.

Passion is an important ingredient in attaining pleasure from any hobby and, while I'm sure it's possible to feel that way about rock climbing, cycling, wine tasting or jogging, I'm just not convinced the same kind of *magic* can be experienced. Not compared to what any keen fisher knows. I'm also passionate about the countryside, music, films and parties, to name but a few additional diversions, yet, my wife and family aside, nothing makes me feel quite so alive as casting a baited hook into the unknown.

Just as a certain song or smell can trigger poignant flashbacks to a joyous moment in our lives, those of us who really understand the appeal of fishing can easily and frequently experience a similar but lengthier high. No alcohol or drugs are required to attain this fantastic, childlike level of elation, just a mesmerising connection with nature – which some of us contemporary *Homo sapiens* seem to have lost.

It's a special kind of bliss that I've been privileged to know throughout most of my life, because I was only five years old when Granddad presented me with a small wooden box that smelled like one of his tins of Bruno, or the tartan pouches of Clan tobacco he sometimes brought back from holidays in Scotland. It was an empty cigar box, with tiny brass hinges and a matching clasp and, even before I knew what it had been used for or was intended for now, I started to imagine all the stuff I could stash inside.

My parents were probably there too, and at least one younger brother, but my attention was firmly fixed on my new possession. I'd somehow been singled out for this unexpected honour, and a present of any kind outside of birthdays or Christmas was a rare treat indeed. Receiving that unexpected gift is one of my earliest memories and, more importantly, it led to the creation of thousands more – all them happy and inextricably linked by water.

As I inspected the box more closely, Granddad explained it was for keeping fishing tackle in, before producing a handful of floats and a few other, as-yet-unidentified objects which were also to be mine. As he handed them to me, he explained that some of the floats were made with porcupine quills, painted bright orange or yellow at their tips, while others had bulbous cork bodies and narrow cane stems. The upper halves of these 'perch bobbers' glowed crimson, like miniature apples glossed with varnish, and they held my gaze more keenly than any Dinky car or chocolate bar.

After carefully placing the items inside, I wrote my name on the lid to prevent anyone else from possibly mistaking it for theirs. For the first time in my life I owned some fishing tackle and, as anyone who is similarly smitten will appreciate, my fascination with that humble collection was soon akin to the allure of ancient Egyptian artefacts to a museum curator.

Over the next few weeks I repeatedly returned to the miniature chest, emptying its contents onto my bedroom carpet to study in more detail before once again putting everything gently back inside. I had no real comprehension of how each item was meant to be used, but they belonged to me and I'd been promised they could unlock hidden wonders from beneath the surface of a pond. What that might mean or feel like in reality, I wasn't sure of either, but I spent many dreamy hours trying to imagine.

CHAPTER 2

Secret Recipes

If fishing tackle is one vital ingredient for a successful day by the water, then bait is surely another. It's no good having a selection of floats, split-shot and a few packets of hooks if you don't have anything enticing to put on the end. And by 'enticing' I mean something that often appeals to both the fish and the fisher, as I would learn shortly before my maiden outing.

My recollection of events between receiving the cigar box and the day I eventually got to use its treasures is now fuzzy with age, like one of the overused cassette tapes that littered my teenage bedroom floor, but

I know it involved many stages of preparation and anticipation. And just a few weeks after I'd taken my unexpected present home with me, I can still remember unwrapping a second angling-related gift, this time for my birthday.

It was a Complete Fishing Kit from Woolworths, although by 'complete' they actually meant a five-foot junior fishing rod and an equally diminutive reel, which came pre-loaded with springy nylon line that looked strong enough to beach a whale. The other accessories were only fit for toys – at least that was the haughty opinion of a boy who had now studied every page of *The KnowHow Book of Fishing*[1] many times over.

By this stage I understood a little about the refined equipment used by serious fishermen and I'd even attempted to make a landing net from an old broom handle, wire coat hanger and potato sack, just as my new bible advised. Besides, I already had my initial collection of more grown-up tackle from Granddad and I now cherished the new rod and reel just as dearly.

That unbreakable length of fibreglass would come to serve me well over several years – everywhere from Sheffield's parks to the North Sea – but, as I eagerly freed it from the plastic and cardboard packaging on my sixth birthday, the real magic still hadn't begun. The true spell wasn't cast until a warm June evening around two months later, when I was driven to Downing Road in my pyjamas along with a rucksack carrying my tackle, clothes and wellies.

It was finally 'Angling Eve' – the first of countless butterfly-inducing nights I've savoured since, when I know I'm going fishing in the morning – and although I was still to bait a hook all those years ago I was already fizzing with expectation. Perhaps I can recall the intense

---

[1] Anne Civardi and Fred Rashbrook (1976) *The KnowHow Book of Fishing*, illustrated by Colin King, Usborne Publishing Ltd.

excitement so clearly due to what happened in the final hour before bedtime.

Having stuffed myself with the usual after-tea treats, I was loitering in the kitchen and watching Granddad rip pieces of stale bread into a glass mixing bowl. It wasn't intended as my final course, but rather to create something that would take on supernatural qualities in my dreams that night. He was making bread paste.

Nowadays some anglers might view this as an old-fashioned bait and its homemade appeal has been overtaken by more convenient and commercial options like scientifically created, heavily marketed and highly effective fishmeal pellets. Yet to a six-year-old lad, around forty years ago, the process of creating this simple substance seemed downright mystical.

First, he added some milk, then a splash of warm water from the kettle, before mashing the chunks of bread into a pulp. Next came a few teaspoons of flour to achieve the right consistency, drawing disapproving tuts from Grandma, before he turned to ask me if I knew what the secret ingredient might be. I couldn't begin to guess, because the *The KnowHow Book of Fishing* didn't contain top-secret stuff, but I quickly learned it was custard powder.

I didn't even realise custard powder existed, but I knew the end product well – and the scent of vanilla, which gently wafted my way as he prised the lid off a tin of Bird's. I watched in awe as he added a teaspoonful of the dry pink powder to the damp mixture in the bowl and it suddenly turned to a more familiar shade of yellow. Then he kept on kneading until he had a stodgy ball and, after adding a few drops of honey for sweetness, it was wrapped in greaseproof paper and stashed in the fridge.

Later that night I lay in my single bed in the spare room, just a few feet from the other one that one of my younger brothers would have claimed if more of us were staying over, and stared up at the polystyrene ceiling tiles in a trance. I tried to picture what kind of fish might like the taste of custard, or what it would feel like to actually connect with one – something unseen but suddenly pulling back like a mild electric shock.

I knew from my research that plain bread paste worked well for roach, chub, bream and carp, but all those species of fish were just hand-drawn illustrations to me. They were yet to be caught or seen in the flesh, although that fact didn't stop their ghosts from swimming around the dark room as I tried to stop fidgeting and fall asleep.

I must have finally drifted off, however, because the next thing I knew, Grandma was waking me with her fantastically bright, almost musical voice. Sunlight was streaming in through the flimsy curtains before she even pulled them apart and I marvelled at the fact it was somehow daytime. Once satisfied that I was sitting up and unlikely to lie back down, she left me to get ready, but before dressing I wanted to take in the new day. Yawning, I leaned my elbows on the narrow windowsill and spent a few solemn minutes looking out at the world beyond.

I peered around Granddad's well-tended back garden, now bursting with blooms of every colour, before checking out all the other, seemingly endless gardens and houses beyond. Eventually my eyes were drawn to the little pond directly below my window and there they remained. Although I may give my young self too much intellectual credit, I'm sure this pause was my first attempt to savour a precious moment before any fishing trip begins – by which I mean to acknowledge and appreciate the fleeting time of day before 'what might happen' is replaced by 'what actually happened'.

The Magic of Fishing

Staring down at Granddad's goldfish pond, assessing the weather and wondering what the day might hold in store would become a small but significant element of my fishing rituals for years to come. I still did it after I passed six feet in height and usually drank a few bottles of beer before wishing my grandparents goodnight, because the fantastic feeling of waking up at Downing Road never diminished.

I still think it's important to enjoy a bit of idealism before every angling expedition – even now, when I'm old and proficient enough to reasonably predict a decent day, or pragmatic enough to know there's more chance of catching a cold. And that first time I greeted a new dawn as a fisherman, or soon-to-be fisher boy, was particularly spellbinding.

The pond's still surface reflected a crystalline blue sky and billowy white clouds, yet when I squinted my eyes and really focused, I could also glimpse beneath. I watched goldfish cruise silently between lily pads like dainty, living submarines and wondered if I would get to see their wild cousins so easily.

Indeed, I may have remained enchanted for some time longer if it weren't for the tantalising movement of those jewel-like creatures. Seeing them appearing and disappearing amongst the pads, captivating to watch even in their modest home constructed of rubber pond liner, created another surge of anticipation that shook me into action.

Once dressed, I bounded downstairs to find the kind of magnificent banquet that Grandma always provided for us, despite Granddad's equally consistent protests that we only needed some toast and wanted to be on our way. There was to be no quick exit and I forced down some cereal, tinned fruit, toast and a piece of cake before she would let me anywhere near the porch.

Only then, fit to burst, could I help Granddad load the car, before we took delivery of our packed lunches and the bread paste. As was her way, Grandma had wrapped everything in multiple layers of tinfoil, kitchen roll, cling film and old shopping bags, plus there was a can of bitter for Granddad and a large jam jar of decanted lemonade for me.

Not exactly standard fare, but she was part of the war generation and lived by the admirable motto of 'make do and mend', meaning that over time the food and drink we took with us became another unmistakable signature of a fishing trip with Granddad.

As the boot of his car gradually filled up, I gawped at an old wicker basket that seemed to contain ten times as much tackle as I owned. Feeling slightly jealous, I learned it also served as Granddad's seat, while I would get to perch on a small, striped canvas chair that somehow smelled simultaneously like a summer breeze and winter mildew.

Finally, just before we set off, he fetched a metal tin from the garage and, after removing its round, perforated lid, I was amazed to see half a pint of writhing, multi-coloured maggots inside. I'd read about these bluebottle larvae and their proven attractiveness to most fish, but that didn't prepare me for the pungent smell of ammonia and sawdust that greeted my nostrils. I tried to hide my mild disgust as he explained they came from a fishing tackle shop and that it was always good to have a choice of baits.

We would start with bread paste, he said, but if we couldn't get a bite, then we had something else to try. And those wise words about always having a few options available formed my first lesson in the endless choices, decisions, adjustments and uncontrollable permutations that can determine the success, or otherwise, of any day spent angling.

Experts have written chapters or entire books on the impact of different baits, floats, rigs, air pressure, moon phase, tackle and tactics, but as we pulled away from the kerb that morning, I cared for none of it. I was finally going fishing and that was all that mattered.

CHAPTER 3

The Pond

My first fishing trip was to a tiny farm pond that was leased by Granddad's social club and, just like a few other intimate destinations I've visited countless times since, it's hard for me to imagine my life without that diminutive pool of water in it.

It wasn't any old pond either, as I discovered after a twenty-minute drive through the outskirts of Sheffield and another mile of rolling countryside. As we turned off a busy carriageway that continued further down into Derbyshire, Granddad slowed his car to a crawl and said, "Read that sign," before adding one of his all-knowing winks.

On turning my head, I was surprised to see we were entering *Moorwood Lane*. Imagine that, I thought, a road named after me, and proclaimed on an official sign for everyone to see. A little further along, as the lane began to dip, I saw a narrow, gritstone cottage coming up on our left. Its sturdy walls were blackened with ancient city soot and it appeared to crouch beside a knot of twisted trees, as if sheltering from a bitter wind.

Even before we drew close, it struck me as lifeless, and over many subsequent years of passing there I never once saw a light on, a window open or any other sign of occupancy. Yet I was told it was home to an elderly lady who owned the pond and rented it to the club for a nominal annual fee, so I sometimes wondered what she, and her seemingly isolated existence, must be like.

Just before we turned into a rough track, I noticed another sign, this time displayed in one of the cottage's lower windows. It was a wooden one, with *Moorwood Farm* spelled out in flaking, sun-bleached paint. A road with my name was one thing, I thought, but now a farm? I asked if we owned it, as I didn't know of any other Moorwoods besides our family, but Granddad was surprisingly vague on the subject.

He seemed to think not, but I'm sure he mumbled something about an old button factory nearby and, as I remember it, how someone related to us was found hanged there a long time ago. He denied any knowledge of that rather macabre detail whenever I brought it up in later life, however, so I'm still unsure of what to make of it. I always had an active imagination, so perhaps this was just another example of fantasy blurring reality, but then he had so many brilliant and *true* stories to tell that you can't really blame me.

This was a man who had extended his brief honeymoon after returning some glass bottles to a corner shop and claiming the few pennies on offer for doing so. Not that he could rent a caravan near Scarborough for a few pennies, of course, but, before he returned to the campsite, he placed them on the first-, second- and third-place outcome of a greyhound race – a 'tricast' bet with extraordinarily long odds – which came good. Grandma may not have approved of this little diversion, but he apparently won enough money to enable them to stay on for another night, which was no mean feat for a young steelworker.

Faded, confused or fabricated memories aside, the name of the house that owned the pond only added to my intrigue on that bright June morning so many years ago. I strained to catch sight of any water as we bumped carefully down the pot-holed drive, but it proved impossible, as our way was bordered by drystone walls, tall banks of nettles and, far above them, a tunnel-like canopy of elms.

Only when the avenue of trees eventually gave way did I spy a second farmhouse, which appeared to be even more deserted than the first. Dilapidated and seemingly abandoned, it had been left to slowly crumble on a broad ledge of land that briefly interrupted the downward flow of the small valley we had just descended. And beside the pile of ivy-clad buildings was a place to park.

"We're here," Granddad announced, and I tried to stay calm by focusing on the impressive view before us. The land fell away steeply – a patchwork of small fields sweeping down to reach to the southern suburbs of Sheffield, which appeared hazy and grey in the distance. A few microscopic glints of glass were the only highlights against a dark, jumbled expanse of buildings.

Lines of traffic were just about visible too, crawling silently along the artery roads like processions of four-wheeled ants. It was an unusual and rather breath-taking perspective of my hometown, and not even the gruesome assortment of real insects smeared across the windscreen could diminish it. I felt like we'd arrived in a new country.

I also sensed something special was about to happen – a sudden knowing that spurred me into action. I clambered out to explore my new playground and quickly decided that no one else could possibly be aware of such a secluded spot, never mind have the right to fish there too. It seemed utterly removed from the noise and bustle of urban life, a secret and wild place where time stood still.

Wood pigeons cooed gently from the tops of the elms and the sound of faraway sheep was also perceptible, carried to my ears on a gentle moorland breeze that smelled of green shoots and bracken. In human terms, however, there was only the two of us, and my companion was a man of few words. Instead, he lit his pipe and leaned against the car for a minute, puffing silently and looking like he felt just as smitten with our surroundings as I.

I didn't begrudge him a brief delay and before long he stretched, popped open the boot and beckoned for my help unloading the gear. I was happy to do so and it wasn't long before we were ready to go, at which point Granddad heaved the straps of his basket and rod bag onto his shoulders, locked the car and patted me on the head, before walking back towards the dappled shade of the rutted track.

We only travelled a short distance up it before turning off, gingerly squeezing between a pair of ancient standing stones that formed a rough stile on our left. There was a broad byway beyond, formed of the smooth, wiry grass found high up in the Peak District. The middle section appeared worn and silky, like the cloth of an old snooker table, which told me there must have been other people here before us, but I still couldn't imagine their company.

Our final destination beckoned us onwards, although Granddad ambled slowly down the gentle slope as if still savouring the journey there. We soon passed a tangled damson orchard on our left, which must have belonged to the eerie farmhouse and been abandoned along with it.

To our right was a meadow of waist-high grasses and wildflowers, while in the shimmering distance I could just make out a peaty smudge of moorland. We pushed on, accompanied by the mellow, hypnotic drone of myriad insects, before I suddenly caught sight of a glassy surface, glinting brilliantly in the sun.

I stopped dead, causing Granddad to bump into the back of me, because *The Pond* – as I would come to know it from that day on – had finally materialised. It was a tiny, triangular diamond, held snugly in the narrow valley and set off by dark green trees that rose up steeply from the far bank. They were squat oaks, bent and twisted as if trying to resist the encroaching heather above, while the grassy front bank was flat, open and bathed in sunlight.

Only a handful of stunted hawthorns grew there, bursting with vibrant leaves and the last few confetti-like flowers of May. As I took in the scene, their faint floral perfume mingled with another intoxicating scent – that of reed-fringed water – and conspired to draw me closer. Once there, perhaps knowing the magnitude of our arrival for one of us at least, Granddad let me stand in silent awe for a minute.

I watched iridescent dragonflies skimming the pool's surface, while incredible clouds of tadpoles drifted below them. The Pond immediately seemed to harbour more life than all the park lakes I had ever visited – and that was before I noticed some slim, piscine shapes moving around towards the middle. They looked like shadowy versions of the goldfish I'd watched earlier that morning, but glimpsing even small fish in this untamed environment felt utterly different.

Granddad spotted them too and pointed with youthful enthusiasm, telling me they were roach and adding that it was a good sign to see so many. This seemingly casual observation was my first taste of pre-cast optimism, which is a potent cocktail of hope, excitement and a touch of superstition that can eclipse even the rose-tinted speculation of Angling Eve.

Such moments of heightened optimism are experienced during many other pastimes of course – take golfers hoping for the perfect round just before tee-off, or the fluttery belief in every football fan's heart shortly before kick-off – but I'm sure anglers feel it most keenly. Pre-cast optimism never dies and continues to outweigh years of experience because occasionally, or even regularly if one's lucky enough, even the most fantastical fishing wishes come true.

It's a contagious conviction and, back then, I could scarcely believe that we'd soon be trying to *catch* fish like the ones we observed. Granddad ushered me towards the narrower end of the pool, on our right, and explained how it had been created a few decades earlier, when an earthen dam was built below a spring that brought water into the valley from the moorland above. As dreamlike as the moment felt, we were now going to try our luck near the spot where it bubbled up from deep underground.

I naturally assumed this was because it was the best place to fish and only during later visits did I learn it was largely for safety reasons, as the water was barely three feet deep. Several years would pass before I was allowed to cast into the 'deep end' by the dam, so I long-believed it must be bottomless in the far corner, beneath the lichen-clad oaks.

The myth was only shattered when I was about ten years old, after I'd foolishly dropped my rod into the water and Dad bravely ventured in to recover it. At the time this seemed a reckless act, but after catching his breath he calmly announced that he could almost touch the bottom, before feeling around for my prized possession with his bare feet. I was overjoyed when he found it, but remember that my relief was tinged with regret – a sudden realisation that I could no longer believe in those fathomless depths and the monsters they hid.

On my first, glorious visit to The Pond, however, my imagination was unencumbered by such knowledge and it was already running wild. Even scanning the surface of the so-called 'shallow end' begged tantalising questions about what might lurk below and I tried hard to concentrate as Granddad gave me instructions on how to tackle up.

First, I threaded the reel line through the rings of my Woolies rod with trembling fingers, before he explained that a porcupine quill was all I'd need for a float. He allowed me to pick one for myself and, once attached to the line, he showed me how to dunk it in the margin repeatedly, adding another split-shot to the line each time until only the luminous orange tip was visible.

"Aye, that's cocked perfect," he said, before demonstrating how to attach a fine hooklength, complete with a size 18 hook, to my mainline. Only when I held it up to take a closer look and the thin golden wire glinted in the sunlight did I notice the strengthening heat on my back. It was a lovely summer's day and I didn't realise or care that cloudless skies weren't the ideal conditions for catching lots.

I was about to embark on a lifetime of learning, new experiences and, eventually, obsession – but, as so often happens by the water's edge, I was entirely caught up in the moment. Granddad unwrapped the bread paste that I'd watched him make the evening before and my hook was soon hidden in a tiny, vanilla-scented blob.

He carefully lowered my rig into the water, just to the right of where I was seated and a few inches from a thick wall of flag irises. The lush, sword-like leaves and vibrant yellow flowers made for an eye-catching backdrop and I watched my bait drift tantalisingly downwards until out of sight, before it presumably came to rest near the matted roots of the reedbed.

He then pushed a metal rod-rest into the ground, which he referred to as an 'idleback', and handed me half the ball of paste. I was advised to scatter some free offerings around my float to attract fish into my swim, before being left to my own devices. I was actually *fishing* and, although he'd only gone a few paces, I soon felt quite alone.

The illusion was only broken after a few minutes, when Granddad reminded me to "watch out for bites," but he needn't have, because my eyes were already glued to my float. It therefore came as a shock when I suddenly realised it was no longer there. I don't remember seeing it go under, but I do recall an initial feeling of confusion that swiftly turned into panic as I decided it must be a bite.

I clumsily lifted the rod tip to see if the culprit could actually be a fish, but unfortunately there was no resistance. There was no sign of my bait either – news of which I relayed along the bank in an awestruck whisper. Granddad chuckled and said, "You've been done!"

He was a patient type, but a touch of frustration became evident as I continued to wave the rod tip above my head and hopelessly tried to grasp my bare hook.

Looking back, this was perfectly understandable as he was yet to wet a line and he'd neglected to explain how I should re-bait for myself, meaning he was soon back at my side and talking me through what to do if my float went under again.

Crouching down, he went over the difference between a nibble and a proper bite, how to strike and then how to carefully play a hooked fish before swinging it out of the water and into my free hand. My young brain was spinning and we hadn't even touched on what I should do if I was lucky enough to land one, but, looking back, I imagine his mind was racing too.

After all, this was his first attempt at teaching a complete novice to fish and, despite all my theoretical preparation, the ramifications of his admirable new role must have dawned on him over the next few hours. A lifetime of finding peaceful solitude or enjoying social outings with his mates from the club was drawing to an end.

From now on, much of his fishing would entail extra planning and driving, endless questions, repeated shouts for help, fiendish tangles to undo and a dramatic reduction in time spent actually catching fish. Such is the difficult path for anyone who takes on an apprentice, but he was teaching me something I would love for decades to come.

My passion was kindled during that first visit to The Pond and while I was still wondering what kind of finned thief had made off with my bait during the previous cast I saw my float bob in the water. Just a nibble I told myself, before it dipped again and then slid away confidently. It was one of the most thrilling things I'd ever seen, and this time I remembered to strike.

Far too eagerly, though, because I actually hooked a small roach of around two ounces and the flexing strip of silver suddenly found itself swinging through the air before either of us had a chance to work out what the hell was happening. I yelled in dumbfounded triumph and Granddad was soon striding back to me, this time with a satisfied look on his face.

I also sensed his pride, especially once he'd managed to catch hold of the tiddler and bring it down to my bewildered eyes for inspection. My first catch was barely longer than his palm and it lay there quivering, gill covers pulsing rhythmically like some marvellous mechanical toy. Even in such miniature form I was struck by the creature's dusky grey back, metallic flanks and pink-tinged fins.

I only had an instant to appreciate all of that beauty, however, because moments later I was being shown how to unhook the fish and return it safely to the water. I slipped my roach back with reverence, watching it hang above my submerged fingers for a second before coming to its senses and darting away. It was gone as quickly as it had arrived but the memory of its capture would never leave me.

I got back to my feet in stunned silence while Granddad quietly wiped his hands with a bar towel, perhaps contemplating the historic nature of my achievement too. Only after a long minute had passed did he pat me on the shoulder and tell me to have another go, which seemed like a rather casual suggestion under the circumstances. The idea of *repeating* what I'd just accomplished seemed a lot to hope for, but I eventually went on to catch several more dainty roach that memorable afternoon.

They were just like peas in a pod yet I revelled in every success and time dissolved away without thought. It therefore seemed like we'd only been fishing for an hour or so when I noticed the sun was somehow close to the treetops opposite. My guide had also started to check his watch a lot, much like a referee in the final minutes of a football match, and although I didn't realise it then, the sight of Granddad frequently glancing at his wrist would come to signal the beginning of the end for most of our trips.

Indeed, the only pain he ever caused me – aside from the fact he wasn't really invincible – was each time he warned me that our time by the water was running out. The close of every little adventure was hard to accept whether we had caught well or not and I always pleaded for "one more cast" while wondering why we had to pack up by 5pm, especially when I'd read that evenings were the best time to tempt big fish.

"How can you want to leave when we're still getting bites?" I sometimes muttered under my breath, but of course I had no responsibilities or appreciation of 'real life'. I hadn't promised my wife that we'd be home for tea, nor had I spent the last few hours getting up and down to extract snagged hooks from my grandson's clothing, or to console him after something more substantial had snapped his line with a devastating rush to freedom.

Back then I didn't care for any of the rules governing adults, although at least now I can appreciate Granddad's many small sacrifices and the endless patience that allowed me to follow in his footsteps. Still, the bitter disappointment of making our way back to the car, my hands covered in slowly drying fish slime and bread paste, was always hard to digest.

It was a lingering kind of sorrow that only began to ease once we'd left the countryside behind – either having landed back to another feast prepared by Grandma, when I would describe my latest successes and savour her exaggerated gasps of astonishment, or on getting home to be distracted by the telly and my family. And no matter how this new fever was soothed, it always returned before long, burning just as fiercely, because I was well and truly hooked.

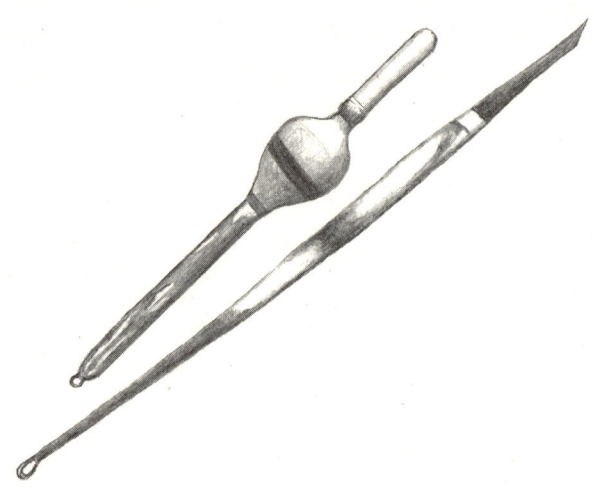

CHAPTER 4

The Apprentice

It was barely a half-acre, yet The Pond loomed large in my thoughts and quickly became the centre of my childhood fishing universe. Granddad continued to take me there once a fortnight over the summer months, and during the first few years of my addiction I never once wondered what it might be like to visit somewhere else or whether fish could be caught in the depths of winter.

It wasn't for me to question why we only frequented Moorwood Lane, or why our trips always began in June and ended in October, because it was all I knew of fishing and everything I wanted it to be. I eagerly read everything I could about my hobby and therefore understood the theoretical scope of possibilities, but I also began to realise the vast difference between standardised scenarios described in print and the infinite variables encountered in the field.

There was no danger of boredom because only the route to our favourite place remained the same. Naturally, The Pond grew more familiar over time, but every visit was unique. The changing seasons always made their presence felt and we ventured down the same grassy path on scorching August afternoons, misty September mornings and chilly October days when autumn winds swept down from the moors and began to strip the trees.

Changes in microclimatic conditions could also alter the mood within the valley many times during the course of a few hours, and I gradually became attuned to these continual shifts – whether a subtle increase in humidity, the first rays of sunlight breaking through on a dull afternoon or the more threatening appearance of storm clouds on the horizon. I also learned how my quarry might respond to localised weather events, although angling is rarely predictable and there were also times when the exact opposite of what I predicted actually occurred.

Delicate floral perfumes and heavier, earthy scents defined each visit too, as did seasonal birdcalls, occasional glimpses of mammalian wildlife and the ripening of grasses in the meadow. Yet reassuring patterns could be found between the corresponding months of each year.

During June and the great tadpole invasion, The Pond always appeared full of a rich brown broth, positively bubbling with aquatic activity. Whereas July and August's algae blooms brought a sultry tinge of green and, as the oak leaves yellowed in October, they once more floated down to settle on a slate-grey surface that could appear lifeless and brooding.

Despite beginning to recognise these natural cycles, and even after casting from the same handful of spots thousands of times, I never started to feel the place could become predictable – not like a Rubik's Cube, board game or Pac-Man – and nor could its inhabitants. Our staple catch remained small roach of the same stunted stamp I encountered on my first visit, but that only meant the surprise appearance of a speckled gudgeon or striped perch was even more notable.

Never mind a rare, enthralling sighting of a large tench or wild carp lurking in the weedier corners. I held no serious hope of ever touching one of those enigmatic creatures and I don't think Granddad did either. He regularly forgot to bring a landing net, such was the level of expectation, although that was largely irrelevant because the hooks we used came ready-tied to flimsy nylon that any self-respecting carp could snap with ease.

My sleep was still troubled whenever one of those leviathans had made its presence known, no matter how briefly, but I tried to accept that catching them was beyond my reach and the next best thing was to see one. June was when most of The Pond's inhabitants spawned, including the few large ones, and sometimes they would remain in an amorous daze beyond the opening day of the season. As a result, they were mostly uninterested in our bait but less wary and elusive than usual.

During these early season visits, with Granddad's begrudging permission, I would sometimes creep round to the far bank on a monster hunt. We were yet to fish over there because I normally had to stay within ten yards of him – a rule he argued was sensible in case I fell in, despite the fact he'd never learned to swim – and that only added to the intrigue.

I would pause upon reaching the narrow end again, now opposite my guardian as he began to tackle up, and check for a final blessing. Once reassured that I wasn't about to get ticked off, I'd move onwards and gingerly crawl through the undergrowth like an ill-equipped Amazon explorer. The scratches and stings were worth it, because not far beyond the clawing branches was a reedy inlet where the water was only a foot or so deep. And there, perhaps just three or four times in my young life, I discovered a fellow visitor.

On each of those memorable occasions I froze in surprise, trying hard not to move and briefly holding my breath after spotting a large tench, almost within touching distance. They were probably resting after depositing eggs amongst the weeds and their broad, olive-green backs almost broke the surface, while their paddle-like pectorals splayed out on either side for balance. A pair of orange-rimmed eyes would then swivel to assess the unexpected presence of a little boy and there we would remain, staring at each other for as long as I could keep still.

Whenever I found one of those cryptic fish lurking there, it would seem impossibly large, but those 'giants' of my childhood were probably only three or four pounds in weight – babies by today's specimen standards, although my best catch at the time weighed mere ounces. So even after finding the hidden channel devoid of life, the memory of previous encounters was enough to make me giddy as I headed back round for the first cast of the day.

The only thing to quicken my pulse more than witnessing a tench or carp was actually hooking one, which did happen from time to time. Then I would feel their terrifying strength for a second or two before the line inevitably parted and sent my float springing back into the brambles behind me.

Those fleeting connections would leave me bereft,

with a strange ache in my stomach that took some getting used to. It was a feeling of loss coupled with a desperate longing to know what might have been and, although it would become more familiar over the years, it's still hard to recover whenever a 'biggie' gets away.

One of my most surprising encounters at The Pond didn't involve a monstrous fish, however, but another angler. It occurred at the start of our second summer there. Over the course of the previous year it had started to feel like our own private estate – an exclusive fishery where the only other guests to disturb our peace were wild animals seeking a drink. On this occasion, though, we arrived to find someone else's car already parked at the end of the track.

I assumed it must be a farm worker or hiker's vehicle and didn't think too much of it, but on our way down to the water I suddenly spied a hunched figure, half-hidden in the gloom under the oaks, and only then did I understand we wouldn't have the place to ourselves. It was a shock to realise we weren't the only fishermen to know about The Pond's existence and I felt surprisingly downhearted at this unexpected intrusion. Although, as we drew closer, Granddad went some way to dispelling my concern by greeting the man warmly across the pool.

"Eh up, Bill," he said. Bill slowly raised a hand, smiling in response, although his eyes, which were partly obscured behind the kind of heavy, black-framed glasses I associated with Eric Morecombe, didn't shift from his float. His other hand remained equally still, clutching an old cane rod like the poised beak of a heron, and I estimated he was a little shorter and rounder than Granddad.

Despite the growing warmth in the morning air, he wore a flat cap and bulky tan overcoat. I watched him suspiciously until Granddad whispered that he was the club secretary and a seriously good fisherman. That piqued my interest and we left our gear in the usual spots on the front bank before approaching his shadowy lair as quietly as possible. Once we were close, I was told to hang back a little while my chaperone crouched beside him and asked if there was "Owt doing?"

Bill confirmed he'd had some "reet nice roach" earlier in the morning and, after a conspiratorial pause, added that he'd "had 'em on stewed wheat." I had no idea what that was, but it clearly wasn't bread paste or maggots and it seemed to work for 'reet nice' fish. My interest grew, and then I was formally introduced and instantly felt the camaraderie most anglers can expect from each other.

He said it was "good to see a young'un 'ere" and then Granddad told me that his friend was one of the few people to have caught a carp from the club's water. I listened in wonder as Bill described how he'd used a boiled potato as bait and fished into dusk one mid-summer's eve, in the very spot he occupied now. He could tell I was enthralled and added that it had taken "an age" to tame the powerful fish. Here was an angler, I thought, who might be even more accomplished than Granddad.

Later that year we arrived at The Pond once more and again found Bill already fishing in the deepest corner. This time, however, he was accompanied by a young lad who, to add insult to injury, was located in one of my favourite swims. He was twice my size and looked like a teenager, so I found his presence rather intimidating. Granddad didn't appear to know him either, but after saying our hellos he turned out to be Bill's grandson and just as affable.

Following a brief chat I mustered enough courage to settle down in the adjacent peg and, despite having achieved some basic competence of my own by then, that afternoon I witnessed my first angling master class. Not only could Bill sit patiently for hours and sometimes catch roach big enough to require a landing net, it seemed his grandson was blessed with similar watercraft, wisdom and skill. The roach he was catching as I tackled up were mostly of the size I was accustomed to, but he swung them out with a frequency I'd never thought possible.

Soon I was getting a few bites of my own and he looked to be using small pinches of bread like me, yet every single cast seemed to result in another fish for my neighbour. As I tried to keep up and managed to winkle out a couple in quick succession, he glanced my way and suggested we should have a match. And this, he explained, meant seeing who could catch the most.

His friendly challenge seemed a little unfair, as he was clearly going to win based on the last twenty minutes alone, but my competitive streak meant I couldn't decline. And in the end it was indeed a thrashing, although I didn't really care because I'd observed an amazing feat of angling taking place just a few yards down the bank.

Despite the fact Granddad and Bill struggled for bites and seemed to enjoy their pipes more than the fishing that day, the boy wonder next to me quickly reached *thirty* roach and still kept going. Only at the end of the day, after I'd had to pack up and then knelt down to watch the demonstration more closely, did he reveal one of his tricks. He wasn't using bread as bait after all, but something called 'teacakes'.

As I recounted what I'd learned in an excited babble, Granddad said it must be the extra sugar and cinnamon that had driven the roach mad. So as we said our farewells and I reluctantly left the young wizard in peace, noting that he was allowed to stay fishing for longer than me, I took some consolation from the fact I'd been up against a new bait with powerful properties. My opponent was also far more experienced, of course, but I vowed to keep learning until I too could catch that many fish.

I kept my promise and did go on to achieve similar feats over the coming years, eventually getting to know every part of The Pond almost as well as my own home. I drew maps of it; wrote down plans for it; dreamed about it; and tried new tactics there – all of which was necessary to occasionally, just occasionally, feel like I knew what I was doing. Of course, I could never fully understand or predict the fish that I yearned to catch, but I regularly started to trick enough of them to impress Granddad.

I slowly acquired more tackle, too, using every birthday and Christmas to ask for any costly items of gear, such as a rod bag or small wicker basket of my own. I re-read books and magazines, asked questions of any anglers we came across on family walks and pestered for more trips. Although I would remain a humble apprentice for many years to come, I began to feel I was on the path to becoming a real fisherman and, more importantly, I hoped to become a *great* one.

CHAPTER 5

The River

I was probably eight or nine when I discovered The Pond wasn't the only place to go fishing. My awakening happened after school on a glorious Thursday afternoon just before the summer holidays, when I jumped off the number 60 bus and immediately spotted Granddad's car outside our house.

I ran down the short hill at the top of our road because its presence was unusual on a weekday. I therefore dared to hope for a surprise outing, but it was only once I'd found him, smoking his pipe in our garden and discussing bedding plants with Mum, that I learned it would be no ordinary trip. Not only was it a weekday and approaching 4pm, but we were going to try our luck at a river.

After I hurriedly changed clothes and fetched my tackle from the garage, we set off on a new adventure.

Granddad told me his old steelworks now leased a short stretch of the River Derwent, which I'd never even heard of, but we would apparently be fishing for its trout and I had definitely read about them.

I speculated they were 'game fish' – usually caught for the pot, on artificial flies, by gentlemen of a certain social standing – and my chauffeur nodded in agreement, before explaining we could fish for these trout with a float and bait because he'd worked for the company for so long. Whether that was strictly true or not I still don't know, because we never saw another angler, bailiff, gamekeeper or indeed anyone during our many visits there.

The journey was slightly longer and even more impressive than the familiar drive to The Pond, and my mind raced with possibilities as we sped over moorland before heading down a winding forest road. Country air rushed in through the open windows and mixed with familiar scents of tobacco, soap and a stash of Opal Fruits in the glove compartment.

We eventually slowed to a more sedate pace before taking a sharp turn down the wooded valley-side. The car tilted unnervingly, such was the abrupt pitch of the lane we entered, and Granddad edged his way down it cautiously before the land levelled out and we arrived at a typically picturesque Peak District village.

As with my first trip to The Pond a few years earlier, I suddenly felt we were drawing close to something special and eagerly looked for a first glimpse of water. My crackling sense of anticipation was soon rewarded and, after turning a tight corner, we headed towards the entrance of a narrow, stone-walled bridge. Its humped carriageway carried us right over the Derwent and for a few moments we were almost completely surrounded by water.

The surface moved like molten metal, tinged with numerous tones of pink, yellow and peachy-orange. In the few seconds it took us to navigate the old crossing, I glimpsed eddies, swirls and boils – gaining a fleeting impression so different from the tranquil, unruffled water I was used to seeing at Moorwood Lane. I'd seen plenty of rivers before, of course, but we were actually going to *fish* in this one.

Once we'd bumped onto a grass verge just beyond the bridge, I also noticed a thick band of pine trees that sprung up a few hundred yards from us, on the far edge of a small field, and snaked away along our side of the river. The darkness beneath their jostling branches was so distinct from the glinting water beside them and added to my growing sense of wilderness.

After Granddad pulled on the handbrake and turned off the ignition, we sat quietly for a minute, the silence only broken by a gentle ticking from the engine. We never felt a need to fill such pauses with small talk and this one was particularly prolonged. It seemed we both wanted to savour our arrival at *The River*, as we would call it from then on, in equal measure.

"Time to use one of your river floats," he said at last, "and I've brought us some bigger hooks tied to stronger gut," which was an old-fashioned word he still used for nylon line. These were small details, but they raised my hopes further because it could only mean he expected there to be stronger, and therefore bigger, fish than we were accustomed to.

I couldn't wait to make a cast, but first, he told me, we would need to find some bait. And as we unloaded our gear, he grabbed a garden spade and a couple of empty compost bags too – essential tools for collecting worms and, soon I would learn, fertiliser for his garden. Indeed, over the next few years, most of our trips to the Derwent involved the harvesting of 'cow muck' for his roses, which made the return journeys particularly memorable.

To get to our ultimate destination we had to squeeze through a narrow gap in the wall and negotiate our way down some daunting stone steps that jutted out on the other side, all while awkwardly balancing tackle on our shoulders. Only once we'd reached the lush turf could we relax, readjust our straps and head for the pines. They separated the river from some neighbouring farmland and that's where the cows apparently lived. Although we never saw them, they liked to wander through the trees to take a drink – leaving plenty of circular calling cards in the process.

Entering the wood was like stepping through an enchanted wardrobe and the air was heavy with pine resin and wild garlic. We moved a little way along the narrow, needle-strewn path, before stopping to dig for worms. Granddad handed them over as he went and I placed them in our maggot tin with the kind of reverence one might hold for the finest frankincense.

He then used the spade to fill his compost bags with dry 'pats', before finally leading onwards. We followed the course of the river and I noticed the narrow tree trunks crowded close to the water in many places. That meant we only stopped again once we'd reached a stretch of relatively open bank that was long enough to accommodate both of us.

For some unknown reason I haven't revisited that spot – a place so integral to my childhood – for several decades now, but if I close my eyes and really concentrate, I can still see it almost as clearly as I did on that first visit. There was a hefty section of felled tree between us, lying parallel with the path, which I soon clambered up and sat astride while Granddad positioned our wicker baskets.

An army of tall pines stood behind and on either side of us, but the view over the water was unrestricted. Granddad mentioned the far bank was inaccessible to anglers or walkers and it certainly looked overgrown and impenetrable, like the mangrove-fringed shore of a distant island.

The ground immediately beneath my feet was bone-dry, cracked in places and riddled with hungry roots. There were a few tufts of grass and clumps of nettles where the dusty earth met the swirling river, however, and the narrow path continued to our right, disappearing into the shadows and onwards to who knows where.

Rust-tinged water swept past us and instead of tadpoles drifting below the surface, clouds of midges whirled manically above it. They caught the sunlight like supercharged dust motes, while alien noises emanated from the trees all around us – unfamiliar birdsong, slow creaks or a sudden clatter as squirrels chased through brittle branches.

I also realised we were preparing to fish at the kind of time we usually thought about packing up. Everything was glowing with an early evening radiance, including Granddad's face as he handed me a packet of hooks before returning to his basket to light a pipe.

After opening the small paper wallet, I teased a neatly coiled length of nylon from one of the transparent leaves within. Then I began attaching it to my main line, which already sported one of the red perch bobber floats that had seemingly been waiting for this moment since the day I got them.

Everything felt right, but after making my first cast I was surprised to see the float move swiftly to the right and then, as the line tightened, swing round in an arc to almost touch the downstream bank. I asked Granddad what to do and he explained I could try trotting, by leaving the bail arm of my reel open and carefully letting line slip off the spool while the float made its way downstream, or, as it was my first time on a river, perhaps I should just leave my rod in its rest and fish close to the bank.

I decided to keep things simple and settled down to wait, but after a while I learned something else about this new kind of fishing: there weren't many bites. The longest I'd had to wait for some kind of action at The Pond was thirty minutes on a frosty autumn morning, but after a good hour on the Derwent neither of us had caught anything or seen any sign of fish.

I started to feel daunted by the sheer amount of water in front of me, and Granddad had to remind me we were trying for bigger specimens. He let out another puff of smoke from the corner of his mouth before telling me to be patient. And not long after those words of encouragement, something happened that could have kept me fishing until midnight.

Without warning, a sizeable trout surged upwards, leaping clear of the water only a few feet from my float. It seemed to hang in the air for a second or two, before crashing back through the surface and vanishing from sight. I blinked at the spreading ripples, still trying to comprehend what I'd seen, but even after they'd gone my reserves of hope were fully restored.

"Did you see that?" I gasped. Granddad nodded sagely and urged me to keep an eye on my float, but he needn't have. The slo-mo action replay was looping in my mind, making me feel almost queasy with expectation. In fact, some years later, I recognised the same, overwhelming sense of tension during one of the classic scenes in *Jaws*: the moment where the cord-like fishing line slanting away from the stern of the boat suddenly jerks taut, as something unseen attacks the bait in the depths below. The reel clicks two or three times before briefly falling silent, making the characters on board, along with the viewers, hold their breath.

My perch bobber was designed to indicate interest from a far less dramatic predatory fish, but time still seemed to stand still as I watched it weaving to and fro. I *knew* something was about to happen – and then I got a bite unlike any I'd seen before. The float seemed to shudder and then stop moving altogether. And it held that unnatural position for a second more, sitting fractionally lower in the water than it should have been, before bouncing twice in quick succession and then moving confidently upstream in defiance of the current.

I shouted for Granddad's advice and he told me to wait, saying I needed to give the fish time to take the worm properly. I felt almost paralysed with the fear of messing things up, but managed to grab my rod just as the crimson float was towed under. Then, seemingly from far away, I heard him shouting, "Strike! Strike!"

I duly struck, but wasn't prepared for what happened next. My rod hooped over and something surged away from the bank with the kind of shocking acceleration I'd only experienced briefly before, after hooking a carp at The Pond.

This time, however, the stronger hooklength held firm and I became conscious of a strange noise coming from my reel. It was the drag – rasping in protest as the spool spun under pressure and gave back line at an alarming rate. This was an unfamiliar feature of my reel that I'd never needed until then, but luckily for me it seemed to have been set at just the right tension for an angry trout.

I hung on, wincing, while Granddad loped over to offer anxious advice as the fish charged further away.

My emotions flipped between soaring hope, that I might actually get to see what was on the end of my line, and painful pragmatism, because surely I couldn't beat something that pulled like twenty roach harnessed together.

Optimism only got the upper hand when the initial dash ground to a halt and I was able to regain some control. My adversary continued to thump and twist somewhere out in the middle of the river, using the current to help thwart any initial attempts to tame it, and the next few minutes felt more like hours.

Only when the trout eventually tired, allowing me to slowly draw it closer to the bank, did my 'gillie' decide to put the net together. As he fumbled and swore behind me, I looked down and saw a series of flashes, still fairly deep down, which confirmed it was the biggest thing I'd ever come close to landing.

My legs felt weak and I hardly dared move until Granddad was back by my side, instructing me to keep the line tight while carefully increasing upward pressure. After a few near-misses, he finally swung the writhing mesh onto the bank with an exultant shout. That's when I could put my rod down and take a closer look – not just trembling, but shaking uncontrollably.

"It's a beauty!" Granddad exclaimed. And it was. Two or three pounds of torpedo-shaped muscle. Its silver flanks were touched with beautiful spots of colour, like random dabs from a paintbrush and, once he'd unhooked it, he handed me the fish using a rag from his back pocket. It was far livelier than anything I'd previously encountered and I struggled to keep hold of it.

As we continued to wrestle, Granddad reassured me it was okay to use a cloth to handle the magnificent beast because, for once, we wouldn't be returning it to the water. Instead, I was informed, it would be eaten. That was news to me and I immediately protested, "But I hate fish!" Which, in one sense, was perfectly true. It's an irony that's not been lost on my family and friends over the years, but the taste and smell of the cooked variety has always repulsed me.

"Don't worry," said Granddad, "you might not like it, but your mum and dad are going to love a bit of fresh trout." And that's when another fact dawned on me: I could take this writhing beauty home. Not to consume myself, but to show my family what all the fuss was about. Here, finally, was proof that I could catch something serious.

It felt like an extraordinary accomplishment and I wanted others to see it too, so agreed we should keep it. He explained we needed to kill the fish humanely and I watched with a mixture of fascination and horror as he gave the top of its head a sharp knock on a nearby trunk. The limp and lifeless catch was then returned to me and I was advised to place it in my wicker basket, before we had time for one last cast.

For once, I didn't care that our trip was nearly over and was content to sit in the gentle warmth of the evening sun and let the drama sink in. In the end, one bite had been enough. I wanted for nothing more and Granddad enjoyed a final pipe while my float returned to its previous place near the bank, swaying there for a few more minutes.

There would be no further action, but I sat patiently and kept returning to the fact I had somehow caught a wild brown trout from this untamed river. Not only that, but soon I would be able to show it to my parents.

Later that evening I was taught how to gut a fish in the sink: first snipping its fins away with kitchen scissors, then crudely sawing its head off with a knife and finally scooping its innards out with my bare hands. I tried not to retch and if I didn't like eating fish before this was probably the point of no return. Yet I was still riding high on the impressed looks and sincere congratulations I'd elicited from Mum and Dad when we arrived home.

Even Sam and Joe seemed interested and answering their questions about how it had all happened felt better than winning any sports day event or pulling off a new skateboard trick. Granddad had listened patiently too, but eventually said goodbye and left me to retell the story over and over while getting some first-hand experience of how an animal becomes food.

That was something most of my friends wouldn't encounter anytime soon, if at all, and I marvelled that only hours earlier I'd seen my fish take another life, as it smashed through the river's surface to devour an unsuspecting fly or minnow. The predator had quickly become the prey and, once I'd finished my gory duty, I noticed the trout's skin had lost some of its original lustre.

The wild fighting machine had been reduced to packaged meat, its platinum scales now appearing a little greyer, and I realised my triumphant feelings had dulled a little too. They were muted by a creeping sadness, and once I'd scrubbed the last scales from my hands and got my pyjamas on, Dad came into my room to find me crying. I was confused and my thoughts were distorting, as can happen in bed, but I was undoubtedly shedding tears for the life I'd taken.

I made a sobbing confession, before he could reassure me that fish don't have the same self-awareness or nervous systems as human beings – plus it had been killed quickly, he argued, and would now provide a welcome meal. So after a few more deep, shuddering breaths I began to take some comfort from that age-old perspective: my trout hadn't died in vain, or without respect. And with a few more soothing words of reason I eventually succumbed to sleep.

Things seemed much clearer in the morning, and later that day I held court in the school playground, explaining to anyone willing to listen what it was like to cast into a river and land a trout large enough to eat. Ben, my best friend, seemed genuinely interested in my latest fishing tale, although, for the time being, I didn't believe he could *really* understand what had happened.

That evening, having barely registered the classroom or indeed any of the lessons about theoretical matters, I witnessed my first catch from The River provide a fine dish for Mum and Dad. After seasoning the fillets, they fried them in butter before washing them down with beer and singing my praises once again. I watched on proudly, steadfastly refusing several pleas to "try a bit" but suddenly knowing what it felt like to be a provider.

Although, I still don't like eating fish and I still prefer to return my catches to fight another day.

CHAPTER 6

Matchdays

I enjoyed many trips to the Derwent over the next few years, which quickly established itself as another sacred place in my life, but The River could never eclipse The Pond, because the experience of fishing them was so distinct.

Hopping off the bus and seeing Granddad's car on a Thursday afternoon meant I'd soon be feeling the crunch of pine needles underfoot, before swatting at midges while waiting for a speckled trout to find my bait. We sometimes caught grayling too – a new and fascinating species with elegant, sail-like dorsal fins – and I began to recognise the calls of moorhens and the gentle 'plop' of a water vole going for a swim.

The Derwent also meant balmy summer evenings that often ended with a cold glass of lemonade outside a moorland pub. We'd take in hazy views over the purple heather, squinting at distant rock edges that seemed ablaze in the hour before sunset, and share peanuts while discussing our earlier fortune. Sometimes Granddad ordered me a 'boy's beer', which some landlords would tolerate back then, and I'd proudly sip at a bitter shandy while perched at a picnic table alongside my beloved companion.

This simple doubling of venues seemed to expand my angling horizon many times over, but The Pond lost none of its sparkle. Moorwood Lane remained synonymous with Friday sleepovers at Downing Road, playing cards with Grandma over a mug of Horlicks and staying up late enough to watch the start of a *Hammer Horror* film. And then I would wake on a summer's morning, relishing another chance to experiment with new tactics at the place where my fascination began.

There's no doubt I could have continued in that simple yet enthralling rhythm for most of my childhood. Call it blissful ignorance, but those two modest waters still drift into my dreams more than any other angling destinations I've known since.

I never grew tired of our repeat visits – at least not for another couple of years, when my laws of physics were again turned upside down. And this time it wasn't merely the discovery of a third place to fish, but a whole new *universe* of possibilities.

It was called Dronfield Woodhouse Sports and Social Club, or DWSSC for short. It was, and still is, based in an unassuming, single-storey brick building about halfway between Sheffield and Chesterfield. Like any self-respecting social club, it offers pool and snooker tables, a darts area, meeting rooms and, despite being located opposite a pub called the Miners Arms, a popular bar that caters for buffets and parties of all shapes and sizes, including the annual meetings of its

The Magic of Fishing

fishing club.

Despite having fallen in love with the club's pond at Moorwood Lane over the previous few years, I was only officially signed up as a junior member when I was about ten years old. I didn't initially appreciate the significance of Granddad's application either – not until I received an official welcome letter and it became apparent that I was also invited to several fishing matches every year.

"Real competition," Granddad said, before explaining that each one promised a day out to a different river or lake, usually during the months of June, July, August and September. Even the idea of trips to unknown fishing venues didn't seem life-changing on the face of it, but by the end of my first summer of DWSSC matches, they'd become like a new religious calendar – one that endures to this day.

In the early years I always started my preparations a few evenings before the big day and then slept at Downing Road on the Friday night. There I'd fill up on pancakes while discussing rumours about where we were going the following morning and soaking up any tips that Granddad had picked up in the tackle shop. I went to bed buzzing with expectation and hoping that sleep would come swiftly, because waking up on matchdays soon became the next best thing to Christmas.

After selflessly rising at the crack of dawn to see us off, Grandma would hand over the elaborate packed lunches she'd prepared the night before, usually with a tutting remark about the poor quality of modern bread. She would then stand at the end of the passage in her quilted dressing gown, resplendent in curlers, and wait to wave us off while we loaded the car and tried to quietly push, rather than slam, the doors shut.

We spoke in whispers because neighbours lay slumbering all around us – their heavy curtains shielding them from the sunlight that crept silently across roofs and turned upstairs windows into fiery rectangles of orange. As we prepared to set off, I often glanced around and briefly considered all the people hidden behind those shimmering panes of glass. I tried to imagine their collective snores, wondering how they could just lie there, oblivious to the enormity of the day ahead.

Although their absence was actually an important part of matchday mornings, because the empty streets always felt like ours alone. Any remaining drowsiness evaporated as we gently accelerated away from Grandma, all of us still waving until well out of sight, and as we turned onto the main road Granddad would unfailingly pat his cardigan pockets to check for his pipe and tobacco – the precise moment I knew we were truly on our way.

Every trip was wonderful – a combination of comforting tradition and so many unknown factors about how things would unfold – but the first match of the year was always particularly exciting. Having endured a long and fishless winter, the June match was like the return of warmth in spring air, or a long-awaited arrival of another childhood birthday.

I began to appreciate every little sign that meant a fresh summer of matches was finally upon us, and the rush of happiness was so intense I can still relive many of our trips in a patchwork of poignant memories. Memories so vivid they make me question how my hair is now grey.

On the way to our rendezvous at the club we unfailingly stopped at a small corner shop located right on the southern edge of Sheffield, just before the border with Derbyshire, where the owner seemed to know Granddad quite well. He was one of the few other people awake at that hour, and discovering there were shops open so early – at least before I started to associate them with laborious paper rounds – made me feel part of a new, grown-up world.

Granddad usually chatted to him about the weather and its impact on his garden, before buying a paper and a pack of Polos, which he'd later share with me to help stave off our pre-breakfast hunger pangs. And while the two men joked over the counter like a scene from *Open All Hours*, I headed to the back of the shop seeking copies of *The Angling Times* and *Angler's Mail*.

They were usually hidden behind heavy piles of *The Star*, *The Yorkshire Post* and *The Racing Post* – fresh off the delivery van and still smelling of damp ink. And while these modest purchases may have seemed like a non-event to the casual observer, as part of our new matchday routine they sent me floating back to the car, lightheaded and fantasising about catching something like the hefty specimens on the front pages.

Fishing always inspires hope – a lovely, uncertain yet wishful belief that today might just be *the* day. And while I have no doubt that golfers, rugby fans and keen flower arrangers can all wake up and pray for a perfect sequence of events, I'm less sure they can touch the all-consuming anticipation of a young angler.

Even after a string of matches ended in failure, the next began with the same butterfly-inducing optimism. Belief surged back regardless of past experience, because success in competitive fishing doesn't rely entirely on countless hours of practice, sound strategy, personal performance and the prevailing conditions. Those things count for a lot, of course, but there's usually a slice of luck involved, too – whether it's a slither or a big old slab.

It's true that anglers who rise to the top of their particular specialism – be it on the match circuit, specimen hunting, fly fishing or the pursuit of monsters at sea – can minimise the need for good fortune with hard-earned skill and instinctive watercraft. For example, several outstanding match anglers have won multiple World Championship medals despite fishing in a range of countries, in wildly differing conditions and against the cream of the crop, which doesn't happen thanks to rabbit paws, four-leaf clovers or shooting stars. Yet luck can *still* play a role even for them.

No matter the extent of one's experience, abilities or gear, there's always the possibility of drawing the best peg, or that a huge, wily fish might just slip up on a difficult day, so I always believed that anything was possible – at least until reality told me otherwise. It was an irresistible state of aspiration that imbued everything and everyone around me with a sense of warmth.

Once we left the newsagent behind and approached the clubhouse, often slowing down to let an old coach complete its lumbering manoeuvres, the sight of familiar figures milling around the car park was the next heartening confirmation that I wasn't still dreaming. As we eased past them to find a space of our own, waving or nodding at friendlier individuals through the windows, I began to understand the meaning of camaraderie.

Some of them were friends of Granddad, retired steelworkers like him, but even the slightly dour-looking characters proved a reassuring or intriguing sight after months of absence – some for impressive fishing skills I'd glimpsed the year before, others for a wicked sense of humour, and one or two for a surprising level of shyness that almost matched my own.

Being reunited with these working-class men, gathered together once more on a summer's dawn, was reassurance that I hadn't somehow invented the previous year's meetings. During the short days of winter, they'd started to feel more like figments of my imagination, but as I saw them again, laughing and smoking in small groups like kids on a dance floor, I felt a unique sense of belonging.

Once we'd parked and unloaded the car, we joined the others to catch up on snippets of news and wait for the last few stragglers to arrive. Then we helped the driver load the belly of his coach with countless baskets, canvas rod bags, waders and assorted carrier bags full of food, bait and beer.

As I pitched in, to the extent my scrawny arms and legs would allow, I realised that I could already pair some of the items with their owners. I didn't yet know their names, but I remembered that a relatively young bloke used a fluorescent newspaper bag to carry his nets, while another member's rag-tag collection of tackle always looked like it only had one season left before everything would surely fall apart at the seams.

I also started to view Granddad in a different light: already my hero, I started to appreciate he was popular amongst old workmates and friends from the social club too. He was never flamboyant or excitable himself, but was often greeted with vigorous handshakes, enthusiastic slaps on the back and genuine grins, while I was the target of much friendly leg-pulling and many ruffles of hair.

"Eh up, it's the young'un, come to beat us all!" some wag would usually roar as I clambered up the steps of the coach, meeting air so thick with cigarette smoke that I had to blink back tears while searching for an empty pair of seats. For many years I was the only child to attend the matches regularly, but I never felt out of place. I only felt privilege and gratitude to be accepted in such an alien environment.

The grandson of Bill, who had amazed me with his cunning use of teacakes a few summers before, made it along on a few trips, but his lack of consistency made me question his dedication to something he'd mastered as a younger boy. He must have been sixteen or seventeen at this point, however, so girls, alcohol and lie-ins were probably taking precedent – pleasurable diversions I couldn't begin to appreciate just yet.

I was happy being the youngest member by several decades anyway, despite the fact it meant I was hopelessly out of my depth, because matchdays were about so much more than winning.

Once everyone was aboard there was a quick headcount and then the coach set off, gear changes crunching noisily and everyone lurching to one side as we rounded tight corners. The banter continued apace, and although some of the language made my face flush and Granddad grumble into his paper, most of the talk was good-natured and innocent enough.

I was fascinated by the strong accents of my fellow passengers, at least compared to what I was used to hearing in my relatively middle-class neighbourhood and school, and initially struggled to follow conversations. Some of the fishing terminology was new to me, too, and it took a while to make sense of phrases like, "Nah then, Joe, tha's been 'ere before 'ant thee, so what's t'best oil?" Which roughly translated to, "Joe, as you've been to this place before, where's the best fishing hole?"

Other common phrases included: "Oh nay-ow, 'ave bin watter-licked!" (Oh no, I've not caught a single fish); "Tha's a reet jammy bastid" (You're a really lucky man); and, "Ave 'ad nowt but bits" (I've only caught very small fish). So not only did I learn more swear words than many of my schoolmates, but I gradually became fluent in northern fishing-speak. It was just another aspect of my acceptance in the glorious world of match fishing and, in later years to come, I started to use it myself, unashamedly turning up my accent whenever north of Newark.

CHAPTER 7

The Mighty Trent

During the first few summers of DWSSC matches, there was technically only one destination involved: the River Trent. Yet, at 185 miles, it's the third longest in Britain and offers so many contrasting features, moods and fish stocks that it can seem more like twenty or thirty different venues. It certainly felt that way to me, back in the 1980s.

It was a daunting river for a young lad to continue his angling apprenticeship: so wide in places that I could barely cast a third of the way across; so powerful I sometimes needed four ounces of lead to hold the bottom; and so untamed that, when in flood, I witnessed everything from mature trees to obscenely bloated cows sweep past in the surging, chocolate-coloured water.

There are also lower stretches where, on certain days of the year, skilled surfers can ride a continuous tidal bore for a few miles upriver. And even on normal days the waterline moves up or down by a few feet during a day's fishing. I was astonished during my first visit to such a place, as the moon's weakening pull revealed a chaotic riverbed of jumbled boulders and glutinous mud where my float had been trotting only an hour before.

Angling in these tidal sections entailed several moves away from, or back towards, the water's edge and, as I became more familiar with the cyclical shifts in the direction of flow, strength of current and water level, I realised the fish were influenced too. They sometimes seemed to vanish completely, leading to hours of frustrated boredom, or suddenly 'switch on' and feed with reckless abandon when I'd all but given up.

Growing up as a fishing fanatic, the Trent was also the stuff of legend, with famous stretches like Burton Joyce, Gunthorpe Bridge and Nottingham Embankment regularly featuring in the library books and magazines I devoured. Visiting some of those places with the club became like pilgrimages for me, because match heroes like Ivan Marks and John Allerton were known to have cast from the same banks that I was now walking.

The quality of fishing was also famous at the time, although there have been equally barren and bleak periods since. Thankfully, many stretches of the Trent have regained their former glory in recent years, often making headlines for specimen fish these days, but I can remember a golden era when the most accomplished angler, given a good peg, could use a fibreglass rod, centrepin reel and simple stick float tactics to catch quality roach, chub and perch from the steady current all day long.

The skylines of many popular stretches are dominated by huge concrete cooling towers of the power stations and, just like some of the well-known weirs, they've always been magnets for both fish and anglers. Warm water was regularly discharged into the river at certain times of day and, particularly in winter, vast shoals of roach or bream could therefore be found residing in these balmy areas – or so I sometimes overheard the fishermen of DWSSC claim, exchanging stories in reverential tones as our coach made its way onto the M1.

The outward journeys were always filled with similar rumours, talk of past glories, opinions about how the river had been fishing and, more importantly, what the day might hold in store. But as we drew closer to finding out, the mood usually shifted, with tall tales, jokes and even the smoke gradually thinning out and replaced by more earnest questions about favoured tactics, baits and 'oils'.

If an intrigued fishermuggle had stowed aboard and remained quietly in the front row, like David Attenborough trying to win the trust of mountain gorillas, these exchanges about the best shade of groundbait or where the freshest casters could be bought would have sounded like the impenetrable mutterings of a secretive sect. Yet within a year or two I started to make sense of it all and tried to glean what I could from those men who shared my burning desire to catch fish.

No hooks would be baited just yet, though. Not until after another important ritual was complete – the eating of a big breakfast. We usually got to our chosen pub at around 8am and much like the corresponding section of the Trent these old hostelries gradually started to become familiar. Some became traditional haunts, while others fell out of favour for a while, perhaps after a change of ownership, only to reappear like an old friend a few years later.

The Magic of Fishing

As we disembarked from the coach and formed a semi-orderly line, shuffling slowly and quietly into a dark lounge that reeked of stale beer and smoke from the previous night's revelries, everyone would stretch their limbs and the humorous chatter gradually resumed.

The subject of fry-ups inevitably came to the fore, and while we queued for mugs of tea, bundles of cutlery in napkins and sachets of ketchup, passionate views were aired about how many sausages were served on the last visit, whether there was genuine HP Sauce available or if the fried bread looked any good.

For a year or two I could only wonder what all the fuss was about, raised as I was on a simple bowl of cereal in the morning. But I again felt like an accepted member of the gang whenever Granddad and I were invited over by two or three members who were already seated and sipping hot drinks.

"By 'eck, tha's growing!" someone would usually exclaim as I shuffled up to the table, while another might ask, "'As tha got any maggots or 'emp with you today, lad?" Not only was I offered plenty of advice at this point, but it inevitably came with a gift: a slice or two of cheap bread from a plastic, mock-wicker basket lined with a serviette.

"Get some o' that on yer 'ook if you want to land a big'un today," one of them would say, at which point the other men nodded and mumbled a collective "Aye" like it was a piece of archaic wisdom being passed down to the next generation for safe keeping. I initially treated it as such too – at least until my fourth or fifth season, by which time I'd heard the same nugget of advice, and failed to catch a big'un with my slice of white, at least a dozen times.

Nonetheless, the pre-match breakfasts gave me the chance to get to know a few of the members better and, although they naturally came and went over the next few decades, many of the earliest characters live on in my memory to this day. In fact, as I somehow find myself well into my forties, there are even one or two characters from the end of my Granddad's era still attending the matches.

People like Mick, who not only still attends most of the matches but often helps with the back-breaking weigh-in process at the end. He must occasionally measure the passing of time by my ageing, just as I do by his, but back then I thought everyone in the club was ancient. Now I'm forced to recalculate and some must have only been in their thirties when I first met them – which naturally makes *me* ancient now, by my own reckoning.

One character still sadly missed was 'old John Swift', as Granddad always referred to him. Like me, John loved fishing the Trent. He was a builder by trade, as was his son, Gerald, who I believe still drinks in the clubhouse, and they both had deformed fingernails that must have been hit with a hundred hammer blows.

Together, they ran the club for a decade or more and, although I liked them both, Swift Senior was particularly memorable. He was a gentle and mildly comical friend of Granddad's, but that's where the similarities ended. John was a bigger man, with even less hair, and I struggle to picture him without a clipboard clutched in one of his meaty hands, smiling and swaying gently in the aisle of a moving coach.

He always wore baggy brown trousers on the matches, which were hoisted so high by a pair of braces that the hems of each leg swung a good few inches above a pair of hobnail boots that might have been of Victorian origin. He was quite hard-of-hearing and also partially sighted, with yellowing plastic hearing aids behind each ear and a pair of glasses with lenses so thick that the 'jam jar' jibe barely did them justice. His eyes appeared so impossibly large through the mucky lenses that I sometimes had to stifle a laugh as he shouted for everyone to "listen up" in a squeaky, high-pitched voice that didn't seem to fit his physical bulk.

Once we'd left the pub and made our way back onto the coach, some still offering earnest critiques of the culinary fare, John had one of the most important jobs of any matchday. As we hit the road once more, he would produce the 'bag of destiny' (that was my name for it at least) and then set about shaping everyone's fate.

It didn't look very grand – a canvas, drawstring pouch of infinite age – but within it were twenty metal discs, each stamped with a number that would potentially make a big difference to everyone's day. This was the moment of 'the draw' and my pulse increased as Mr Swift slowly made his way from the front of the coach, stopping at every row of seats until he reached me and Granddad.

Every man took their turn. Some appearing to make silent prayers, others trying to break the tension by prophesising doom before rummaging in the bag for a few seconds. Only after withdrawing their hand would each learn where they would spend most of their day, or even, potentially, their chances of winning.

Some stretches of the Trent featured permanent pegging and there might be a few famous or in-form spots that some of the men hoped to pick, but for the majority of our matches everyone's destiny remained a number, and nothing more, until we reached the bank. Yet the disc selected didn't merely dictate where one would fish; it also determined one's immediate neighbours, how far one might have to walk and, on a well-known stretch, whether one was likely to struggle or not.

So, despite many members attempting to appear nonchalant and keep a poker face, it was obvious the draw was a moment of serious tension. John announced and then recorded each result as he went, sometimes prompting cries of envy – "Tha's a reet jammy beggar!" – if a peg was known to be a 'flyer'. Or less encouraging words – "Tha might as well leave yer tackle on t'coach and get thee sen down t'pub" – for anyone deemed to have been less fortunate. Either way, John scribbled on his clipboard and moved ever closer.

My own fate lay with Granddad during the first few years because he always insisted that I be placed in the next peg to him – presumably so he could scoop me out with a landing net should I fall in – although he also let me reach into the bag when it was finally our turn. He congratulated me no matter what number came out and a problem only occurred if both adjacent pegs were already taken. In those rare cases, Granddad simply gave John a wink to ensure things were suitably rearranged.

Despite my irrepressible excitement as I groped around in the bag, Granddad was one of the few people who didn't really care what came out. He ideally liked to avoid a long walk but was generally anticipating a day of peace and quiet with his pipe, friends and grandson.

Competitive success was bottom of his priorities and he never won a match while I was fishing with him. Not that he was a bad angler. For example, he claimed the overall OAPs' prize at the end of one season – filling me with pride as he stepped up to receive a small trophy at the annual prize-giving night.

The idea of winning was never far from my thoughts, however, and by the time we reached the river I was usually gripped by a familiar fever, sitting quietly but starting to project everything I'd read, heard and planned onto the next six hours of the day. It was hard to stay calm as everyone filed off the coach for a second time and we reversed the earlier tackle-loading process.

By this stage *most* of us were feeling a heightened level of anticipation. Even if not for the fishing, when the weather was fair we could at least guarantee a pleasant day in the countryside. The old-timers always brought a few beers, a newspaper and some kind of hat to shade their eyes – or potentially pull down over their face should a quick nap appeal.

The coach usually parked on the edge of a field at the end of a narrow lane, in which case the dew-laden grass was soon flattened by busy feet and chaotic piles of fishing tackle. As the men gathered their belongings, some lit another cigarette or casually stretched their arms with a yawn, but most looked like I felt inside – mildly agitated as they hastily searched for a missing rod bag or keepnet. I could tell they were just as eager to get going, assess their peg and start thinking through tactics.

There was never any danger of someone mistaking my junior fishing basket for theirs of course, but I still felt a little anxious as I searched for and then moved my prized collection to one side. I was keen to avoid any possibility of a mix-up and only then was I happy to help Granddad assemble his possessions too.

My adrenaline often spiked again once that was done, because it was usually possible to smell, if not see, the Trent. A mesmerising blend of fresh air, verdant bankside vegetation and molecules of river water – usually combined with the unmistakable contribution from a nearby herd of cows and Granddad's first pipe of the day – always ignited another burst of mental fireworks.

Yet before any further exploration of our surroundings was possible there were a few more crucial tasks to complete. The first was a confusing and occasionally tense discussion about exactly where we were fishing, because in those days it wasn't always straightforward.

If indeed permanent pegs existed, they were often marked by weathered wooden stakes with barely legible numbers that had faded over countless seasons. Or sometimes a bailiff had pegged out cardboard squares the evening before, some of which had been blown away or trampled on by thirsty cows.

Not only that, but if we'd booked halfway along another club's stretch of water, we often needed to start from a random peg number, like 118, which would be our peg number 1. Therefore, if someone had drawn peg 19, they first had to do some basic maths before setting off in search of 137. Simple enough for one of us perhaps, but multiplied by twenty or so men, some with hearing difficulties, and we often ended up sounding like excited traders on the floor of a stock exchange.

And before we even embarked on these confusing treasure hunts – sometimes only to discover the numbers stopped after the first ten pegs – we also had to estimate how long it might take to get there and tackle up. In other words, when the match should start and who would take the silver football whistles that would signal 'the off'.

I always wanted the earliest start possible, which would mean less of a nerve-shredding wait to cast in, but now I can understand the older members wanting plenty of time to heave their heavy tackle across two fields, over three stiles and down a perilously steep bank.

Only once the small army of anglers had dispersed and everyone found their allotted place did the final pre-match ritual take place, which typically lasted around an hour. This encompassed an assessment of one's peg, the making of strategic decisions, plus meticulous tackle and bait preparation – all before several whistles blew in quick succession along half a mile of riverbank.

Unlike many of today's matches, involving manmade fisheries with neat wooden platforms, tight pegging and neatly mown banks, it wasn't uncommon for each swim to be a fair stroll from the next. They were often found below tall earthen banks which had been eroded by countless winter floods, while mature willows and hawthorns screened the view to either side. All human life was hidden and, other than a quick chat with Granddad just before the start, I soon became completely absorbed in my temporary home.

Being back on the Trent soon started to feel almost spiritual – just as thrilling as sitting in the Kop at Hillsborough, only with the tribal buzz and roar of the crowd replaced by utter solitude and anticipation. And perhaps that's why I can still recall the final few minutes before those matches so clearly. I can easily picture myself, like an archived out of body experience, seated on my small wicker basket, dangling welly-clad feet in the water and waiting to hear the whistles. Usually staring out across the vast river and sometimes feeding a few maggots to any swans that cruised over to investigate my presence.

Large industrial barges or pleasure craft often ploughed their way past and created a series of surprisingly violent waves that washed ashore a minute or so later. If they caught me off guard, they could steal a bottle of lemonade or upset a bait tub that I'd balanced on a nearby rock – which was a devastating start, but part and parcel of fishing the Trent.

As were sheep grazing the far bank, or tall reeds continually shifting in the current downstream from where I waited, rustling gently and whispering promises of the fish they might harbour. In those moments, just before the start, I again believed anything was possible. I felt born to catch fish and felt sure that today would be the day I proved just how good I'd become.

Indeed, when I think back to those distant days, the facts of what happened next are almost irrelevant. Although there were occasions where the fishing gods smiled down on me and I caught a few fish worthy of a landing net, the angling itself was a bit like opening presents on my birthday – no doubt the pinnacle, but never quite as magical as the excitement beforehand. And certainly not when things didn't live up to my expectations.

Reality rarely respected a young boy's daydreams, and by the time the whistles blew for a second time – a sound I hated in all but the most miserable of weather – several hours of concerted effort usually concluded with some degree of disappointment and frustration.

With the benefit of hindsight, a long string of failures simply made my determined pursuit and eventual attainment of success all the more poignant, but every time one of those early matches ended I knew there was nothing more I could do. My previous belief fell away, as it did for all but a lucky few. Like me, once they'd packed up and shifted their gear to the top of the bank behind them, most of my fellow members idled on their baskets in quiet contemplation, perhaps eating a leftover sandwich or enjoying the last drop of tea from their flask.

Those retrospective lulls didn't last long though, because soon it was time for the concluding 'weigh-in'. Granddad and I left our gear behind and followed the growing tribe of men as they moved from peg to peg.

They weighed each angler's catch before returning the fish to the water and scribbling a definitive figure on the sheet attached to Mr Swift's clipboard.

This process still heralded some excitement for me, even after a poor day, as we re-joined our comrades and I absorbed the emerging tales of good fortune or woe. Much like weary fans of a mediocre football club, poor matches were usually derided as 'inevitable' – even by cocky types who'd predicted success just a few hours before – while the rare days when most people had caught well were discussed with giddy delight.

The fortuitous few who seemed likely to take the top spots – and who often came from a familiar and talented pool – usually respected the feelings of others and maintained a humble posture. They received any plaudits with good grace and were happy to explain their successful tactics to those who inquired, myself included.

I admired their modest manner, although some well-deserved pride was still evident on their faces and it was a half-hidden feeling of jubilation I longed to experience for myself. Especially when I knew the fish in my own keepnet wouldn't be troubling them.

The weigh-in was the final judgement. Where previously there were only names and peg numbers next to a blank column, there now developed a clear story of who had succeeded, who had struggled and who had nodded off for a couple of hours. Granddad was only mildly interested in the outcome while I strained to see each entry, steadily building a picture of the day in my mind.

A place in the 'frame', or top three spots, was seemingly always out of my grasp, and would remain so for years to come. But the consistent performers only strengthened my belief that I could keep improving and eventually prevail. Until that day arrived, I had to console myself by explaining which baits I'd used to achieve most of my bites – to Granddad or anyone else willing to listen – as we slogged our way through the field.

When the sun was still shining with a late-afternoon intensity, we disturbed countless butterflies from the long grass and felt the heat on our reddening necks. The walk back always seemed twice as long as the outward journey and my heart often ached like it did on the final day of a family holiday.

I silently wished we could extend our stay just a little bit longer or, better still, somehow travel back through time to start over. All good things must come to an end, however, so after taking a last, wistful look at the river, I found myself beside the coach again.

If we were among the first few to arrive, we usually caught the driver sat in a deckchair, reading *The Daily Mirror* and having one last smoke – probably relishing the final moments of peace before the rest of his charges returned. And if he was friendly, looking up to acknowledge our presence and enquiring about our luck, I guessed they were probably a fellow angler. They were the ones who usually got the most tips in the cap we passed around on the way home anyway.

As Granddad and I climbed the steps once more I was always struck by how remote the morning suddenly felt. That was usually the dominant thought going through my mind as everyone else joined us and got re-seated. Some would fan their faces with newspapers while others smoked a roll-up and listened to the football results being relayed through tinny speakers.

I often fell into a trance, lost in my own world, and the spell was only broken when John Swift stood up to shout, "Right, gentlemen!" And once having everyone's attention, he always announced the top three places in reverse order – adding some ceremony, if not tension, to the news.

We generally knew the outcome by then, but still gave the winners, and John, some rightful respect. Each name, placing and weight read out was met with a ripple of applause and a few warm words of congratulation. Or if someone had achieved something exceptional it occasionally merited a few cheers.

Granddad unfailingly let me sit next to the window for the homeward journey, where I'd pull down the peak of my baseball cap and rest my head against the warm glass. Despite numerous bumps in the road I always fell asleep for an hour or so, before waking up groggily as we pulled into the car park at DWSSC.

With my skin glowing from lengthy exposure to the elements and head aching thanks to mild dehydration, plus several unconscious thwacks against the coach window, I then had to accept the day was over. All that was left to do was wearily go through the motions of unloading the coach again, which I did in zombie-like fashion.

Some of the men were still upbeat and talked about cold pints in the club, but I was far too young for that and Granddad also had to accept our destiny was Downing Road, followed by my house. It was an unavoidable return to the suburbs, weekdays and normality.

After saying our goodbyes we drove away from the club, winding down the windows to escape the stench of our slimy nets in the boot. And in those subdued moments only one piece of knowledge could raise my spirits: another matchday was over but I could soon start planning for the next.

CHAPTER 8

Friendship

Despite its significance, I can't recall much about the period when Ben, my best friend at junior school, eventually caught the bug too. He probably can't either, because tennis was his first love and it seems he fell into fishing much like he once fell into the Trent – without warning and to my great surprise.

I suppose, like any young lads growing up together, we simply tried to share each other's interests. We already lived five minutes apart, attended the same school, Scout group and Sunday morning football team – and I probably joined his tennis club around the same time he became a member of DWSSC.

Ben's application must have been made possible through the sponsorship of my granddad, yet I don't remember a single conversation about it. As we turned ten, he'd never been fishing with me and didn't own any of the angling books I'd studied so carefully. I'd never tried to convert him, either – or anyone else for that matter – so I can only assume the involvement of parents, who often work in mysterious ways.

What I *do* remember, through the immense fogbank of time, is the day I unexpectedly discovered that he was also a budding angler. I was at Ben's house one summer weekend and we were both bored, lounging about inside and talking the usual nonsense about who would win in various hypothetical fights, when he casually mentioned he had some fishing tackle outside.

I thought he must be winding me up, but sure enough, after we'd ventured outside and into the gloomy garage, I spotted a black and white fibreglass rod and a wicker basket on the oil-stained floor. The basket looked well used, like mine, and had been passed down by his granddad.

Until then I hadn't known anyone other than Granddad who shared my passion, but that afternoon it was as if Ben had received a visitation and was suddenly a believer. Yet if I fast-forward to our many waterside exploits over the following years, the process by which he got there is missing. Logic says he must have had some guidance, written or otherwise, and he surely struggled to master the basics like casting, tying knots and playing a fish, just as I had, but in my ageing memory bank it's as if we somehow skipped all that.

All that mattered at the time was I'd gained another competent fishing companion and the fact he happened to be my best friend was a bonus. Of course I'd like to say I took him under my expert wing, patiently passing on my hard-earned knowledge like a Jedi master, and maybe Granddad managed to do that without me noticing, but the important fact was I suddenly had a mate who understood the magic too.

Ben has a great sense of humour and we both share a gambler's appetite for risk, so during countless trips together I learned about another side of my hobby: the endless opportunities for mischief and mayhem in the great outdoors. Strong friendships are cemented with laughter, shared experiences and, in our case, pushing our luck to prove respect, bravery and loyalty to each other – or what other people might call stupidity.

We both loved to catch fish and if bites were forthcoming we'd happily spend a day in the pursuit of them – swapping tips, offering encouragement and competing for the biggest catch. Yet on quieter trips, when bites failed to materialise, our focus quickly faded and attentions turned to storytelling, boasts or silly dares.

One such gamble involved my friend's favourite fishing float and took place at one of several former industrial ponds lying along Sheffield's leafy Rivelin Valley. We'd been dropped off on a misty autumn morning and weren't having the best of luck: not only were the fish not playing ball but, as we sat either side of an old sluice gate and bemoaned the lack of action, Ben's float parted from his line thanks to a mistimed cast.

It landed on the water's surface just a few feet in front of us, which didn't seem like a big deal, but as we went to grab the landing net and rescue his treasured crow quill, a sudden gust of wind helped the surface tow drag the float back towards us – quicker and quicker, down into the overflow between our feet. Too slow to react, we watched helplessly as it caught momentarily against the old stone sill before tumbling into the darkness below.

We were both irked by the misfortune, but I could tell Ben was a little upset too. Just like one or two of my own floats that were still originals, handed down from Granddad and associated with numerous special catches, my mate had just watched a bit of family history disappear to God-knows-where.

I felt desperate to help as we both knelt and peered into the algae-plastered opening, which was only about three feet wide. As our eyes adjusted to the murk, we began to make out a short, slimy slope that led to the top of a downward shaft, constructed of crumbling Victorian bricks and studded with small ferns.

"Well that's it," said Ben, with a resigned sigh – and so it seemed. We even returned to fishing, after he'd half-heartedly found another float and been through the rigmarole of tackling up again, but if there's one thing guaranteed to fire up a friend, it's a moment of need. As we sat in silence, reflecting on his loss and the continuing absence of any bites, my gaze kept drifting back to the drain.

"I reckon I could get down there," I ventured after a few minutes. "Don't be daft!" was the sensible response, and I was probably only half-serious at that point, too, but the idea was out there and now there were two pairs of eyes distracted by the gloomy hole that had stolen his cherished possession.

"It can't be that deep," I said after a while, reasoning that the wooded bank behind us only fell away by fifteen feet or so, before becoming lost in a tangle of undergrowth that stretched down to a stream below, "and your granddad gave you that float."

The silence hung between us for a few more minutes, until action replaced words and bravado overcame caution. We were back on our knees again and peering into the darkness when, without warning, I lowered my legs and then my torso into the opening, relying on my elbows to keep my shoulders and head just above the ground – and water – while feeling around for some kind of purchase for my feet.

My back momentarily rested against the sloping entrance of the drain and a continual sheet of water soaked through my jeans in an instant, constricting my chest with its sudden chill. Turning my head to take in this new and unplanned situation, the sight of the pond's frigid surface just behind me was enough to unfreeze my lungs and make me gasp for air.

I was starting to feel a bit panicky, but just as I reminded myself that I still had the option to retreat, I registered a flicker of admiration on Ben's face. Then my wellies found an unseen but reassuring ledge to take some of the weight off my arms. And from there I was able to astound him, and myself, by ducking my head and shoulders below to investigate further.

I surveyed the old shaft and saw there were several bricks that protruded from the otherwise vertical surface by an inch or two. Their placement initially seemed quite random, but they soon began to look like tempting hand-holds on an unconventional climbing wall, which was enough to sway me.

"I'm going in," I announced, before edging my way down more carefully than my dramatic statement had implied. Ben watched me disappear with a mixture of fear and fascination, urging caution but willing me on now that I was committed. Once below the entrance slope, I held onto its slippery ledge with grim determination, lowering my legs further down and eventually finding one of the uneven spots where I could just about place a foot.

After a precarious descent I felt relieved to reach the bottom, crouching down to peer along another narrow and fairly lengthy tunnel that led the water away from the pond at a right-angle. And there was the float! It had snagged in a tangle of twigs, waterweed and other debris, allowing me to grab it with ease – and a rush of delight. Our bad luck had turned and, not only had I survived a journey into the underworld, I'd found my prize within seconds of arriving there.

I clutched the painted quill, grinning, and considered my options – which didn't seem obvious until I saw the proverbial light at the end of the tunnel. I suddenly realised the exit looked to be twenty feet away and appeared to be unobstructed by any grate or bars. As I made my way along the tight passage in a crab-like shuffle, I couldn't be sure, but it dawned on me that I might have been able to get in this way too.

Perhaps I could have strolled down the slope from the dam and found my way into the drain without the need for any perilous climbing or a cold soaking, but that would have been too easy! I thought of Ben's admiration and the encouraging words that I could still faintly hear coming from above and, with only a twinge of shame, reasoned there was no need to shatter the illusion of my daredevil stunt. After all, I hadn't *known* there was a less daunting way in and I'd still taken risk for our friendship. The fact I would survive to tell the tale thanks to a more casual route out was mere detail.

My mind made up, I continued gingerly down the passage until I reached the end and, once I'd emerged into daylight, I found myself still hidden behind a wall of dense vegetation. Having the element of surprise helped to keep the nature of my escape a mystery and, after a few, long minutes staring into a now eerily silent sluice gate, Ben was amazed and somewhat relieved to see me again as I reached the top of the bank, bedraggled and muddy.

I held the float aloft and we high-fived in jubilation. A torrent of questions followed as Ben inspected his reclaimed possession, wanting to know how I'd possibly found it in the dark and then managed to get out in one piece. I soaked up the appreciation and explained in a false-modest mumble about the treacherous climb down, a narrow, spooky tunnel, and how I'd searched around in the black water before eventually fighting my way out through an army of stinging nettles.

And that's how little legends are born – at least between a pair of ten-year-old, fishing-mad boys. Fairly small risks, foolish though they sometimes were, eventually became epic deeds – tales to be retold and reimagined with other friends, even when we were old enough to do it in a pub. Despite Ben's undoubted intelligence, he never once questioned my version of events or thought to investigate how I'd miraculously reappeared. He may well have guessed the truth anyway, but to unpick what happened would've broken the illusion.

Our shared hobby afforded us many such opportunities for childhood misadventure and when we weren't playing tennis or football, building tree houses or making rafts, catching fish became our number one quest. For a while Ben and I were equally enthusiastic as well – at least until our mid-teens, when it became apparent that he was seriously good with a racquet. We eventually took up golf for a couple of years, too, and shared mutual interests in girls, music and other sorts of 'clubs' as we got older, but I'm getting ahead of myself.

While still young and innocent enough to not take ourselves, or indeed anything else, too seriously, we formed the Attic Angling Society. I don't remember when exactly, but it involved a solemn founding ceremony with handwritten rules and the repeating of Scout-inspired promises to do our best and dedicate ourselves to fishing. The AAS only had two members, of course, and its meetings were sporadic – taking place in a 'secret' part of the attic at Ben's parents' house, where we believed that only us kids could squeeze through a tiny hatch in the wall.

There, under the dusty eaves of the roof, we placed some old rolls of carpet, a notebook for recording our catches, a plastic fishing trophy and, on one memorable December get-together, a bucket of sawdust in which we hid a few cheap purchases from the tackle shop in order to hold a festive 'lucky dip'. Ben now lives in Texas, and whenever we get a rare chance to see each other, and stroll down memory lane over a beer, the mere notion of a lucky dip involving five or six items which the contestants had just bought themselves still brings tears of laughter.

Still, our mutual devotion to fishing certainly helped us refine skills and broaden our experience. We routinely begged parents for lifts and began to take part in a few competitions outside of the DWSSC calendar – often between ourselves, or sometimes involving Granddad during a weekend caravan trip. On a few occasions we even entered 'proper' matches with the Scouts that involved 50 or more young anglers from around the city.

One such event remains a private joke between us to this day, thanks to the hype that began when our local troop was honoured by a visit from the rather humourless and intense match-organiser a week before the big day. Once he understood our level of dedication, he took Ben and I to one side and promised great things would happen during the forthcoming trip.

Like some Bible Belt preacher with a strong Sheffield accent, he wound us up to fever pitch, extolling the potential of the venue beyond our wildest dreams and almost guaranteeing success. He explained the match would be held on the River Witham and involve more than a hundred competitors, so we quickly realised this was serious stuff.

He even went on to claim that, "If you get the preparations right, you lads can expect to catch bream the size of dustbin lids." We nodded along rapturously, trying to imagine landing a fish the size of a dustbin lid, while he added that we should bring plenty of sheets of newspaper in order to subdue the countless eels we would also encounter. "They won't stay still unless you do," he explained, "and the winner will need to unhook each one quickly, get his bait back out there and catch the next one."

Naturally we talked of little else during the following school week and I dutifully collected several copies of *The Star* from Mum and Dad. I also invested in a large bag of brown breadcrumbs and tried again to picture a bream so big that I'd struggle to fit it in my keepnet. Ben patiently tied lots of spare hooklengths, as he'd been led to believe many would be destroyed by the savage eels, and we enquired about recent match reports from the Witham in Oakley's, our local tackle shop.

Our only doubt was whether we were skilled enough to win the contest on virgin territory, pitched as we were against so many other juniors from all over Sheffield, but when the Saturday morning finally arrived it was largely irrelevant. As several coaches convened in the Lincolnshire countryside, ninety or so young lads were faced with the most extreme weather I've ever attempted to fish in.

Several sturdy fishing umbrellas were buckled or lost to the river that day. I remember holding onto mine for dear life at times while being buffeted with gusts of wind so fierce that waves broke with flying white foam all along the river. My sheets of newspaper lasted less than a minute in the lashing rain, but of course I didn't need them anyway. No one did.

Not a single fish was caught throughout the entire match and even if we did get a few bites we didn't register them because our rods were continually buffeted about or occasionally swiped off their rests. The adults raced up and down to check none of the participants had been blown into the water and the final whistles could barely be heard over the ceaseless howl of the storm.

Peace only returned once all the sodden, shivering and fishless Scouts were back aboard the coaches. There wasn't much joking and some needed consoling after losing or breaking expensive bits of kit, but it was an experience we'd never forget. And from that day on, Ben and I always uttered the immortal words, "bream as big as dustbin lids," whenever we heard something that sounded too good to be true.

One of the last times I remember fishing with him – before he was gifted a racquet restringing machine for his bedroom and became almost completely dedicated to tennis – was on another day of tricky weather conditions. Not heavy wind and rain on this occasion, but a late-October morning when the air temperature hovered around zero and the hard ground glittered under a cloudless sky.

Despite the mean forecast, we'd decided to make a final visit to Worsbrough Reservoir, near Barnsley, before counting our season largely over. We needed three buses to get there and hoped our dedication would be rewarded with some good fish, but we hadn't counted on thin sheets of ice forming in the margins, which had seemingly sent all the fish to sulk in the deepest reaches of the lake.

It was unbearably cold, and as we sat on our plastic seatboxes, hunched and blowing into our hands, we quickly finished the crisps and chocolate we'd bought at the bus depot and realised there was no chance of catching anything. As always, only a complete lack of hope could stop us giving it a go, but within a few hours we retreated to the relative shelter of a concrete wall, stomping numb feet, rubbing aching arms and cursing our luck.

It never took long for such dejection to turn into creativity, however, and before long we were proposing various dares in exchange for the remaining cash in our pockets. All kinds of suggestions were made, each with a price to reflect the perceived level of risk or embarrassment – ranging from using each other's backs as target practice for our catapults and heavy balls of sticky groundbait, to making unbreakable promises to ask certain girls out come Monday morning.

It was a test of twisted imagination and dark humour as much as bravery, and the idea that grabbed Ben's attention was him going for a swim in the icy reservoir. The simplicity, immediacy and outrageous nature of the suggestion was right up his street – despite the fact we were old enough to know about hypothermia and there was no one else around, such as a group of mates, to witness such a stupid act of bravery.

It was just the kind of foolhardy thing we did to keep ourselves entertained when the fishing was off, and we quickly settled on the princely sum of £2. Ben dutifully stripped to his pants before hobbling about on the stony shoreline like some bizarre character from *Monty Python*. He needed to find a spot deep enough before making his way in and I still fancied my chances of claiming the money.

I guessed he would 'bottle-out' as soon as he felt the water, but to my utter amazement he eventually plunged in and started wading frantically away from the shore. He kept going, too, moving further down the stony lakebed and getting surprisingly distant from where I stood, slack-jawed and wide-eyed, until he was right up to his neck.

Gasping, coughing and spluttering as any remaining warmth was stolen, he floundered about for a full minute – probably to avoid any accusations of an aborted mission – and then half swam, half stumbled his way back to dry land. After racing towards me like a theoretical finish line, he grabbed his clothes and started to demand his winnings, forcing words out between violent fits of laughter and shivering.

We naturally had no towels, so he did his best to dry himself with his clothes, before pulling the jeans, T-shirt and jumper back on in a desperate bid for comfort. And as soon as he'd achieved that, we realised he needed to get indoors, and soon. I felt a jolt of fear as we tried to pack up as quickly and calmly as possible, noticing that Ben's face was turning a worrying shade of blue and the humour had gone from his voice.

He complained his hands were completely numb as he fumbled to break down his rod and it took some assistance from me before we could leave. The worry bloomed in my belly as we clumsily climbed the steps by the dam wall and attempted to jog towards the bus stop, repeatedly dropping things and having to circle back.

In the end, we were incredibly lucky that our heated transportation came along after a short wait. Buses were unpredictable at the best of times in those days, but it suddenly felt something of an emergency and I remember the surge of relief as a familiar shape rounded a distant corner and made its way towards us.

By the time we boarded a second bus, back in the city centre, my friend was looking less likely to need urgent medical attention and we began to laugh again. Indeed, the remainder of our journey was put to good use: crafting explanations for Ben's parents and embellishing every detail of what he'd done in preparation for many classroom retellings the following day.

As a parent, I now struggle to condone or celebrate some of our hijinks, and I'm more likely to wince when considering the possibility that my son or step-children might attempt anything so daft. Swimming in a big lake, miles from any help, was a risky thing to do at any time of year, never mind in October with a ring of ice in evidence. It's not something I would recommend to anyone else but, rightly or wrongly, Ben's dramatic dip – done for nothing more than childhood respect and a couple of quid – soon became enshrined with the rest of our fishy tales.

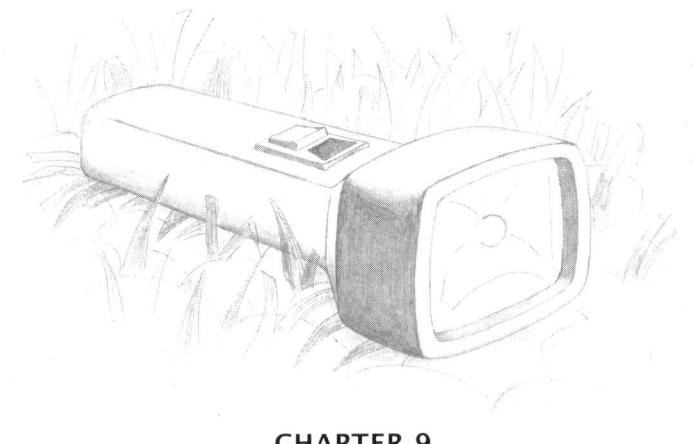

CHAPTER 9

Into the Dark

As we entered Devon, caravan in tow, Grandma offered me another wine gum from the passenger seat of their car, and I again marvelled at the lack of competition for it. My siblings were absent and as if getting a head start on the rest of my family wasn't exciting enough, we were heading to a campsite near Coombe Martin that had its own lake.

Granddad had suggested we get there before everyone else so we could try the fishing, and the idea of several consecutive days on the bank had been fuelling my fantasies for a fortnight. The match outings with DWSSC had introduced the concept of a whole day dedicated to angling, but this holiday would allow me to *live* by the water's edge for nearly a week.

He'd also mentioned the possibility of night fishing, or at least continuing into the first hour of darkness, which I knew was when the big ones were supposed to come out of hiding. And once we'd reached our pitch and seen how close it was to the lake, I was in heaven.

As we surveyed the modest expanse of muddy water and I wondered what it might contain, the clamour of excited kids feeding the ducks or playing hide-and-seek in the nearby undergrowth became more distant. I was mesmerised, lost in thought and desperate to give it a try, but first we had to set up the awning and make camp.

Once we'd established our base and wolfed down some Spam and salad for lunch, we nipped out to a nearby tackle shop for some maggots before eagerly organising our tackle and telling Grandma she knew where to find us if we were needed for anything (though what that might be I couldn't think). We sat side-by-side on a small dam wall and were soon casting our porcupine quills in unison.

The next few hours were actually unremarkable as far as the fishing was concerned, but I didn't mind because we were on holiday in Devon, enjoying the fresh air and trying our luck at a new venue. We eventually caught one or two small fish and got enough bites to keep us interested, but not enough to resist Grandma's shrill calls to come and get our tea a couple of hours later.

I tried not to fidget and joined any conversation politely, but as soon as we'd eaten I rushed back to the pond, leaving Granddad to follow at a more leisurely pace. I loved the fact there was no tedious drive, no need to stop for bait and even our rods were already set up. It was all new to me and more wonderful than I'd dared to hope.

Just a few hours later, I became aware of another significant first. It was starting to get dark and we were still fishing. Granddad wasn't looking at his watch or telling me to have a final cast. Instead, he started talking in a hushed voice about how our chances would start to increase as the sun went down and the big'uns should come out to feed.

His confidence was infectious and my excitement only grew. I also became aware of many subtle changes taking place around us. The young kids who'd plagued us with questions during the afternoon began to drift back to their tents and caravans, the still air began to cool and deep shadows formed beneath trees that loomed over the far margins. It was also getting hard to see my float only a rod-length out.

Perhaps after seeing me craning my neck, Granddad made his way over, his pipe-bowl glowing like a miniature brazier, and handed me a small packet that contained a mind-boggling trick I'd never seen before. Inside was a short plastic tube about the width of a drinking straw, which appeared to contain a clear liquid. He told me to bend it until I heard a snap, which was the sound of a tiny glass partition cracking open. Only then were two chemicals allowed to mix and react – astounding me as a green glow lit up my palm.

Next he showed me how to attach the disposable isotope to my float tip, thereby turning it into a tiny beacon that would soon be hovering above the water's surface like a firefly. By the time we were both fishing with mesmerising, chemically powered floats, it was noticeably darker. Peace descended around the lake, with most of the campers playing cards behind curtains, drinking in the bar or taking a stroll along the seafront.

Squabbling coots were settling down for the night as well, their incessant daytime racket replaced by gentler noises like the harmonious hoots between two unseen owls. I could hardly believe we were still fishing and the nocturnal transformation felt complete once a shimmering moon rose, ghost-like above the opposite treeline. Its soft light betrayed the flitting, near-silent flight of bats, which continually swooped along the lake's surface in search of insects.

The fantastical sights and sounds were almost enough to distract me from the task at hand, but not even owls, bats or an unearthly glow at the end of my line could dispel my longing to catch something special. Staring at the float for more than a few seconds began to play tricks on my eyes and soon it was swaying, dancing and bending against the black surface, but I merely rubbed my eyes, squinted harder and willed it to go under.

Granddad smoked contentedly and the only other light came from the moon above, or a few bright chinks from caravan windows behind us. Distorted conversations and muffled laughter drifted through the night air and Grandma visited briefly with a flask of hot chocolate. I couldn't have been much more content, but one fundamental thing was missing.

I began to question how it was even possible for a fish to find a bunch of maggots in the pitch-dark water, but my prayers would soon be answered because a nocturnal hunter had locked onto their presence. It took a long moment to register my float was gone and, much like the lingering white spot one sees after being blinded by a torch, I was sure I could still see my phosphorescent indicator.

Deeper and deeper it went, until all was black, and only then did I come to my senses. I made a belated, tentative strike, expecting to feel nothing but connecting with something lively and almost frantic. It felt sizeable, too, and the fact I was playing it with no way of seeing my line, and therefore no way of telling where it was going in relation to me, was an unnerving experience.

Granddad was soon marching over to offer encouragement, and after seeing the powerful, stubborn resistance for himself, I could tell he was also intrigued. There were no searing runs like a carp or trout usually made, but my rod tip jagged over repeatedly as the fish made its bid for freedom. The fight was unlike anything I'd felt before and it was some minutes later before the landing net was readied – when our weak torchlight picked out the first ripples that told us I was finally getting the upper hand.

"Easy does it," urged my guide, but I nearly panicked and dropped everything when I saw what had just broken the surface and was still causing the continual thumping sensation down the rod. It was a writhing eel – dark along its back but shimmering, almost white, along its sinuous flanks – and although its head was coming towards me it continued to swim backwards with determined, snakelike waves of its body.

Although only a few pounds in weight, it was a good two feet long and the first of its species I'd seen in the flesh, let alone caught. As it loomed out of the darkness it looked more like a mythical creature than a freshwater fish I'd read about in the comfort of my bedroom, filling me with uncertainty.

Granddad seemed somewhat disgusted by this unexpected vision, too, swearing and predicting it would be the end of my fishing for the night. I didn't initially understand why that should be, but once in our landing net the eel began to coil endlessly round my line, coating everything in a thick, gelatinous gloop and tying both itself and my rig in knots.

I was both fascinated and perturbed, requiring the net's nylon mesh to keep any kind of hesitant grip on the writhing creature. Once I'd done so, Granddad managed to remove the hook and the eel slithered out of my hands, dropping unceremoniously onto the bank and escaping back to the inky water before we'd a chance to do anything.

"Well that's that, then," said Granddad, and I noticed my tackle was indeed beyond repair. I'd even lost my glowing isotope during the chaotic battle and Granddad's earlier prediction had proven correct. He congratulated me on a unique capture, however, so I soon accepted my fishing was done and pulled my basket over to his, babbling about how hard the eel had fought and how much slime was still on my hands.

He decided to have one last cast himself and, despite all the commotion, our night was capped off when he also had a bite and struck into something solid. The battle was far less dramatic but the result was one of the most impressive fish I'd ever seen. It was a deep, bronze-sided bream of around four pounds, which lay still across his lap for a few moments as Granddad let me admire it. Perhaps not quite the size of a dustbin lid, it was still the biggest fish I'd ever seen my idol land.

CHAPTER 10

Ghosts

At the outset of our lakeside camping holiday in Devon, my knowledge of ghosts was limited to what I'd gleaned from a much-loved book about myths and monsters. Sandwiched between chapters about Nessie and the Abominable Snowman were some equally fascinating pages on supernatural phenomena.

I'd spent hours studying grainy images purporting to show a graveyard visitation, or the blurry face of a long-dead queen peering from a castle window, but hauntings couldn't have been further from my mind over the first few days of that trip. We spent more time fishing than I previously thought possible – so much so that Granddad began talking whimsically of beaches, piers and pubs.

I liked those things too, but reasoned there would be plenty of time for them once my siblings arrived.

Until then, I'd be satisfied casting from the same patch of bank until the moment they dragged me away. So it therefore seemed serendipitous when Granddad found a way, or rather a person, to take me off his hands for a bit, while keeping both of us happy.

Nowadays, some might raise an eyebrow at his solution, but this was an era of much greater trust between strangers, and anglers start with more faith in each other than most. During our time on the campsite, Granddad had begun chatting to a fellow fisherman called Steve, who was probably in his early thirties and was on a week's caravan break with his wife.

They were soon on friendly terms, but on the third and fourth days there was no sign of our new pal. Not until the second evening, when he reappeared and found us in our usual spots before letting us in on a little secret. He told us he had discovered a pair of little-known ponds nearby and not only had he been fortunate enough to stumble across them, he'd also gained exclusive permission to fish there. This explained his recent absence, because he'd apparently become infatuated with the place.

Steve said the pools were located in the grounds of a stately home called Buzzacott Manor, but reckoned they hailed from even further back in history. He thought they were likely created as stew ponds to feed the inhabitants of a monastery believed to have originally stood on the site. And my initial interest turned to fascination when Steve described the wild carp he'd observed on his first few visits, including an overnight session just twenty-four hours earlier.

He had begrudgingly returned to the campsite after only managing to land a single fish, which was one of the smaller ones he'd seen, but not before witnessing a couple of carp he estimated to be "at least three times the size". He described them as cunning, slate-backed submarines that had sucked up every grain of sweetcorn he'd offered them – except the one with his hook in it – and wistfully recounted how one giant must have weighed at least fifteen pounds.

I instantly caught the fever so evident in his voice, speaking of little else as Granddad pulled me away and explained that our new friend had been asked enough questions for now. But the next morning, on our way back from the site shop, we stopped by Steve's caravan to say another hello. We found him hunched intently over a bucket of water, testing a ruse he'd dreamed up overnight to outwit the carp of Buzzacott Manor.

He showed me a large hook, onto which he had nicked two grains of normal sweetcorn and another one that he'd hollowed out, meticulously replacing the kernel with a tiny piece of buoyant dog biscuit. I'd never come across such a scientific approach to fishing and marvelled as he showed me how the cluster of grains sank slowly and naturally in the bucket. He explained how the fragment of biscuit counteracted the weight of the forged hook and was convinced that it would fool the wisest, and therefore biggest carp.

He said they had hoovered up his bait many times the day before, but immediately rejected it – blowing everything out in a split second because it behaved in a subtly different way from the other free offerings. I found it hard to comprehend that any fish could be so smart, and I think Granddad was utterly bemused, but I *had* read about the crafty nature of carp and I'd certainly never managed to land one myself.

These stew pond fish sounded trickier than most, despite the fact they had seldom, if ever, encountered a modern angler before, so Steve's story – and his clever attempt to write a new chapter in it – had me enthralled. Granddad must have seen the way I hopped from one foot to the other, asking even more questions and making suggestions of my own, so by the time we left for our caravan he'd agreed that Steve could take me with him when he returned for another go.

Not only did I suddenly have access to a private fishery, an expert guide and the loan of some stronger tackle, but the plan for that evening was to fish until midnight. This was when Steve felt convinced the carp would lose some of their instinctive caution, but staying by the water so late would make my first night-time fishing expedition, when I encountered the scary eel, seem like child's play.

I could barely wait for the day to pass – just like Granddad, who would finally get to spend some time with Grandma and do pretty much anything he liked other than look after me. After what seemed like an eternity, I was eventually dropped back at Steve's with a few sandwiches and an extra jumper. Already beside myself with excitement, I helped him load the car with tackle, folding chairs and a few tins of sweetcorn to keep myself distracted. Then we waved goodbye to his remarkably forgiving and patient wife, before getting on our way.

After a short drive towards Combe Martin we turned into a narrow track with a half-hidden, weathered sign for the manor. I never got to see any buildings, though, because we stopped halfway along the driveway, just above two narrow, weed-choked ponds that lay in a small hollow circled by mature trees. They were well hidden from the main road and indeed from anything else that might indicate which century we were in.

It was a late-July evening and the air was humid as we stepped out of the car and onto sweet-smelling grass to assess the water. There were no signs of fish to be seen, never mind big carp, but Steve seemed unfazed. He emptied a tin of corn into a plastic bait tub and then produced a fresh loaf of bread, proposing that he would try his new, critically-balanced bait on the lower pool, while I should try a piece of floating crust on the upper one.

They were only separated by a narrow strip of land about ten feet across and he explained we would fish back-to-back, thereby ensuring he was close by if I should need assistance. And although I was initially disappointed that I wouldn't get to try the dog biscuit trick for myself, I soon cheered up when he said he'd caught his only carp, so far, on floating crust. *Any* carp would do for me, which was an almost mythical species of fish back then and certainly one I'd never believed I could catch until that evening.

As we approached the lower pond, I saw its banks were covered with spiky tussocks of common rushes and the earth had a slightly marshy feel underfoot. Steve began to move even more slowly, creeping forward in a stealthy crouch and gesturing for me to follow in a similar fashion. We edged towards the water like two cats on the prowl and eventually moved onto our bellies, ignoring the seeping damp from the sodden ground while peering expectantly over the side.

I'd never approached a swim with such reverence, but soon realised why my guide was being so careful. Almost directly below us was a circular opening in an otherwise-dense forest of lily pads and submerged pondweed, through which I could see the bottom of the pond as clearly as if I was looking through the side of an aquarium. The depth must have been six or seven feet, but what little open water existed was as clear as tap water and unlike anywhere I'd fished before.

Steve pointed to the patch of clay below, which was

around three feet across, and explained it had been grazed clean by feeding carp over the previous few days. There was no evidence of them now, but he reached into his tub and gently scattered a few yellow grains into the clearing, just a rod-length from where we lay. We watched as they drifted down, some catching in tendrils of weed but most arriving on the bottom like tiny landing craft on a distant planet.

Nothing stirred and Steve whispered that we should get ready to fish, so we pulled away from the edge and made our way back to his car, which was on higher ground and still bathed in mellow evening sunlight. I was soon furnished with a strong rod, plus a reel spooled with thick nylon that seemed more suited to the sea, but Steve reminded me that carp fight like demons and the vigorous plant life in those pools made landing such fish impossible without the stoutest of tackle.

There was to be no float, just a size 6 hook carefully tied onto the end of my line. It seemed almost comical in size compared to the fine-wire models I was accustomed to using for maggots and bread paste, and only when I was shown how to impale a thick chunk of crust did it seem less outrageous.

"A big bait for a big fish," said Steve, before showing me how to dunk it in the margin to gain more casting weight. After flicking it out beyond the nearest patch of lily pads, he encouraged me to ease it back gently until it rested against the furthest edge, thereby keeping most of the line hidden. Now my buoyant lump of bread would remain there for as long as it took, hovering in the surface film and hopefully proving irresistible to a giant lurking in the cable-like stems below.

After getting me started, Steve was keen to manoeuvre his own carefully prepared bait into position, which he did with a look of intense concentration that I would come to recognise on the face of anyone with a carp obsession. He tightened the drag on his reel and said that, once it went dark, he'd need to detect any bites by holding his line and feeling for any plucks or, better still, a steady take. And I would need to do the same – holding the line between my thumb and forefinger while also listening out for the 'slurp' of a carp taking bread from the surface.

Relying on these senses, rather than sight, would bring a whole new dimension to fishing and it wasn't long before I got my first taste. As the sun sank lower, the heat diminished slightly and we were joined by more bats wheeling and dipping over the surface. As if their dusk feeding activity were a trigger for the scaled residents beneath, we started to see evidence of underwater movement too.

Lily pads began to tremor and even bunched together in places, stirring violently as sizeable creatures began moving through them. And once the sun had disappeared completely, leaving a ruddy streak across the west, the first slurps could be heard. They unfortunately weren't for my bait, but Steve explained it was encouraging proof that carp were on the move and starting to suck at water snails or other aquatic morsels near the surface.

I spent the next hour or two desperately hoping that one of those feeding fish would take my bread, so only when that began to feel unlikely did I notice it had become much darker and eerily quiet. Almost as if someone had flicked a switch, the fish stopped feeding too, sinking back down and leaving both of the ponds utterly silent.

Steve seemed lost in concentration and I became conscious of the fact neither of us had uttered a word for quite some time. We were nowhere near the bright lights of a big town or city and as I looked around me the murk seemed impenetrable. The night was perfectly still and a rising mist carried the intoxicating scent of water mint to my nostrils. I could just about make out the seated figure behind me and felt around on the soggy ground for my torch.

Just as I wondered whether I should switch it on, or break the silence with a few pleasantries, Steve spoke up at last. "You know, John, one thing I didn't mention about this place is the ghosts," he said, which was the *last* thing I expected to hear. I could only respond to his rather nonchalant statement with a nervous laugh, but he knew he'd grabbed my attention.

Turning to face me, he continued in a conspiratorial whisper: "I saw them the other night. I think they were spirits of monks who used to fish here, just like us, but hundreds of years ago." Then he paused for effect, before continuing, "They appeared like glowing figures, several of them, just for a minute, and then disappeared – probably back to wherever they came from."

"I don't think they meant any harm," he added, as if that should comfort me. I shivered, clutched my torch and felt a sudden urge to be back in the warmth of my grandparents' caravan, playing a game of blackjack for matchsticks and eating toast. Steve then went quiet again, possibly not realising the impact he'd had on his young charge.

I looked around in all directions and tried to pierce the gloom, but I couldn't even make out the car anymore. I was lost for words and we fished on in near silence for perhaps another twenty minutes, although my sense of time was heavily distorted with so little to disturb the cloying atmosphere.

The sky gradually clouded over further, hiding the stars and making the air feel even heavier. It seemed almost liquid against my face, while a low mist now shrouded the pond in front of me. The water was barely visible beyond the end of my rod, but I could just make out the point where my line entered the surface, now that my eyes had grown accustomed to what little moonlight penetrated any breaks in the cloud.

I was actually considering whether I would prefer to finish our trip right then, if it were up to me, when Steve croaked "John!" with such urgency it sounded more like a shout. I nearly jumped out of my chair and when I swivelled round towards him I could vaguely see that he was pointing across to the far side of the pond. He jabbed his finger in that direction repeatedly, his face pale and hazy in the mist.

"Look! Look over there," he hissed. "They're back." I scanned the wall of blackness, trying to understand who 'they' could possibly be, but the penny dropped when I saw them for myself. There was nothing solid to see, certainly no living person, and it would have been impossible even if Granddad had been stood on the opposite bank, but the one thing that can overcome darkness is light – and I gawped in bewilderment as several glowing figures seemed to hover near the ground, twenty or thirty feet from us.

They pulsed with a faint luminescence that appeared to come from within or around them and my skin crawled as thousands of hairs stood on end. I continued to stare across the water, squinting to try and make out what was really there, but I knew without anyone needing to utter another word that 'they' were the ghostly monks that Steve had told me about less than half an hour earlier.

"Can you see them?" he asked, sounding as incredulous as I now felt. And I nodded dumbly, continuing to watch as three or four columns of something – be it mist, smoke, or the spirits of ancient monks – continued to sway and shift with a gentle, unearthly light.

I can't easily explain why, but after a minute or so, and even while Steve continued to mumble words of astonishment, I began to feel a sense of calmness growing inside me. Perhaps I realised that I was privileged to be witnessing something I'd never expected to see in my wildest dreams, or even in my nightmares for that matter.

The strange lights didn't seem to be moving towards us or posing any kind of threat, so I sat still and observed, remembering Steve's earlier reassurance that he believed they meant no harm. And we were both still frozen in amazement, watching the barely distinguishable shapes when, just as suddenly as they'd materialised, they faded for a second or two, before disappearing completely.

All was dark once more and only then did fear return. I started to feel panicky and wondered where they'd gone, or more importantly if they might reappear much closer. Yet before I could express my concern or ask Steve what the hell was going on, I realised he was laughing gently and making his way over.

It wasn't a patronising laugh, just a sign of his amusement – and no small amount of genuine wonder – as he crouched down to try and explain what we'd just experienced. Or at least what he *guessed* we'd witnessed, which he referred to as will-o'-the-wisps, or marsh lights.

He spoke with genuine respect for my goosebumps and reiterated that he couldn't be sure, but he thought the luminous pillars were the same thing he'd seen during his most recent visit. I questioned how he could've stayed the whole night there, alone, after seeing something like that, which still feels like a valid question all these years later, but he ignored me and continued to explain his theory.

He said that, after checking the following morning at dawn, he estimated the lights had appeared over some particularly swampy ground on the other side of the pool – an area of stagnant water and rotting vegetation where marsh gases sometimes escaped from ancient beds of decomposing matter. "The idea is," he went on, "that when these natural gases mingle in just the right quantities and atmospheric conditions, they can start reacting with each other.

"It's these chemical reactions that can create billows of bioluminescence in the night air," he concluded. Much like the one I'd seen in my miniature isotope earlier that week, I mused. He admitted that he'd joked about seeing ghosts because the conditions had felt just like those when he'd first watched the strange phenomenon, adding that he'd heard similar tales from regular nocturnal anglers.

He apologised if he'd scared me. Then, just as he was telling me that the theory behind will-o'-the-wisps had never been proven, and therefore they *could* have been the ghosts of friendly monks after all, a distinct slurping noise emanated from the water in front of us. Having almost forgotten we were still fishing, it took both of us by surprise and sounded like a small kid trying to get the last dregs of a milkshake through their straw.

No sooner had Steve stopped talking, cut off mid-sentence by the unexpected disturbance, my rod was heaved round and the reel hissed as something tore off at a ferocious pace. I had just enough sense to grab the rod's handle before everything could be pulled in, and then leaned back against a tremendous surge. He slithered back to his chair, grabbing for his torch, while

I heard the pool's surface heaving somewhere out in the darkness, as a carp thrashed its tail and attempted to get deeper into the weedy sanctuary below.

"Flippin' 'eck," Steve gasped, reappearing at my side and shining a beam across the mist, trying to make out where the fish might be. "Keep it tight," he urged, and I leaned back even more – as much as I dared without breaking the rod, which was now curved into a semi-circle. The straining fibreglass still thumped occasionally as the carp continued its bid for freedom and any remaining worries about ghosts were quickly banished.

Instead, I began to tremble in fear of losing that fish – the first carp I'd ever hooked to remain attached to my line for more than a few seconds. Thankfully, after several nerve-shredding minutes, the strong nylon sliced through the clustered stems and I was reconnected to my adversary more directly.

It now raced around in the short stretches of open water and sometimes made deeper dives with a defiant power that put even a brown trout in the shade. The reel kept conceding line just as I felt it must surely break and Steve implored me to maintain pressure. On and on went the battle and I endured another five minutes of anguish before feeling a modicum of control, which is when he finally readied the landing net.

He advised me to take my time as he tried to track the action with his torch and we both waited for the old warrior to tire. Eventually, it was beaten, turning on its side and slowly sliding over the net-cord, before Steve lifted the mesh around a long, solid mass that was partially obscured by pondweed.

I breathed a sigh of relief and immediately felt exhausted, realising that no fish had tested me like that before. Then my helper gently lowered the bulging net to the turf and we eagerly fell to our knees on either side, before carefully pushing the tangle of weeds away to reveal a stunning carp that dwarfed anything I'd caught before.

The 'wildie' lay gulping air in the torchlight and I knew I was in the presence of something from a whole new league of piscine majesty. Its armour-like scales were the size of one pence pieces and its tail looked to be at least the size of one of my hands, if not both. Its back was graphite-grey, fading to chestnut-brown, and almost flawlessly smooth, while its belly was pale and butter-coloured, punctuated by paddle-like fins tinged with pink and orange.

As I gazed down in disbelief, drinking in every detail, I fancied its eye appeared to hold some kind of intelligence or attitude, which reminded me how difficult Steve had been finding them to trick. I marvelled that I'd actually landed this mysterious creature myself – something that had felt untouchable until the moment it noisily took my bait from the pond's surface.

We sadly didn't have a camera with us, or not one with a flash, but Steve was able to weigh my catch and confirmed it was eight pounds exactly – a decent wild carp for anyone, and a truly amazing one by my standards. Only then was I encouraged to try lifting it for myself, straining just long enough to appreciate its impressive bulk, before lowering it back into the water's edge.

I cradled it there for a while longer and wondered if I'd ever catch another fish quite as handsome. I couldn't imagine so and didn't want to let go, but the carp had other ideas and kicked its tail defiantly, giving me a small soaking as it went.

All that remained were a few droplets of water on my face and a thin sheen of slime on my hands. It was gone, but the images and feelings of its capture stayed with me. Not only had I fished for carp in the dark, but I'd actually hooked, played and held one of those wily fish that I'd heard described with such respect the day before.

As I sat back down, legs still trembling, Steve gave me a congratulatory handshake before turning the torch on his watch. "Just past midnight," he said. "I think that's enough excitement for one night?"

CHAPTER 11

The Dynamic Duo

Damflask Reservoir covers more than a hundred acres and is eighty feet deep in places, making it a beautiful or intimidating sight depending on the prevailing conditions. Over a million gallons of peat-tinged liquid is contained by a sloping dam wall that was built over the ruins of a village destroyed in the great Sheffield flood of 1864.

One balmy evening in the 1980s my dad was picking his way over the rock-strewn shoreline, looking for me. He was actually walking along some exposed lakebed, perhaps because being nearer to the huge body of water helped him feel a touch cooler. As he scanned the horizon, the reservoir was still evaporating and being consumed by the city at an alarming rate, thanks to an enduring heat wave that was now in its third week.

He had just passed the sailing club, feeling mildly frustrated because it had been a good twenty-minute drive to get there and he'd already been walking for a further ten, when he noticed a lone fisherman walking towards him on a path higher up the slope. Dad changed tack and, when they were only a short distance apart, veered up onto the track and greeted him, before asking whether he'd seen two young lads who'd also been fishing.

"Oh aye," replied the man with a knowing smile. "The dynamic duo," he said, jerking his thumb over his shoulder before wiping sweat from his brow. He confirmed we could be found, still fishing, just a bit further along the shore, adjusted the strap of his rod bag, bid my dad a good evening and trudged away towards his car.

I only know about their brief exchange because Dad was still chuckling about it – and our new moniker – when he eventually found Andy and me a few minutes later. Indeed, if it weren't for that typically dry quip from a fellow Yorkshireman, he might have been more irritated with us for not being at the pre-agreed meeting place at the allotted time. But he was still amused by the friendly yet sarcastic suggestion there might be anything 'dynamic' about the combination of his twelve-year-old son and Andy, his new, fishing-mad mate.

We were packing up hurriedly by the time Dad found us, but had admittedly lost track of time because we'd caught so well that afternoon. That was a rare event at Damflask – for many experienced anglers, never mind young lads – and our success was largely owed to the man he'd just met.

The witty stranger was actually Andy's uncle and earlier that afternoon, by some good fortune, he'd found us on the vast expanse of water and decided to give us some tips. With hindsight, he'd probably been pointed in the right direction by Andy's dad, Peter, who had dropped us off around lunchtime, but even so he wouldn't have known which direction we'd decided to take or how far we'd walked since waving goodbye.

Once he'd located us, Andy's uncle had kindly spent a few hours examining our rigs – pointing out their relative lack of finesse and making all kinds of subtle alterations that seemed a bit pointless at first but then seemed to double the number of bites we got – before offering a similar critique of our casting, feeding and striking techniques. Only once he'd miraculously improved our catch rate, and made me question everything I'd previously believed, did he get to fish for an hour or two himself.

Watching him out of the corner of my eye I was reminded of the time I'd seen a teenage magician catching endless roach at The Pond – and knew I was once again in the presence of someone who really knew what they were doing. It wasn't intimidating or discouraging, however, because the advice he'd already given us meant that all three of us were enjoying a fantastic afternoon's fishing. And even when he packed up and left us to it, I felt a new confidence and appreciation for the finer details of hook choice, shotting patterns and accurate feeding to coax the nomadic shoals of roach into action.

The Flask, as it's known by locals, could be even more daunting to fish than the Trent – thanks to its sheer scale, the way the wind often whipped up waves along the exposed shoreline and the fact that the fishing was generally difficult too. Still, it became a regular haunt for Andy and me, and our friendship grew over many hours spent fishing there. We also had two sets of parents to badger for a lift and the fact Andy's dad liked to wet a line himself meant he sometimes came with us.

The huge reservoir was somewhere I never fished with Granddad, however, and by the time Andy and I were getting to grips with it he was a bit too old for the long walk down from the road anyway. Or indeed for the faff of first needing to buy a ticket from a machine that seemed to be located well away from where most people wanted to fish. So over the next few years it became somewhere I associated with Andy and Peter, or sometimes Ben, and also the water where I took my skills to a whole new level.

I will be eternally grateful to Granddad for introducing me to fishing and teaching me the basics, never mind for all of the wonderful memories we created together. But the second chapter of my angling apprenticeship began in a fishing tackle shop in Crookes, which has sadly long since closed, while the 'dynamic duo' were drooling over unaffordable gear.

Dave, the owner, knew us quite well by then and liked to pull our leg, but this particular morning he asked where we were off to and when we replied, "The Flask," he nodded at a newspaper article pinned to a noticeboard by the shop door. "You want to try out for the Juniors," he said. "They're 'aving a trial on t'Flask next weekend."

We sidled up to the board and read the article, which confirmed there would be an open trial for the Sheffield Juniors Fishing Squad and anyone under the age of sixteen was welcome to come along and try their luck. We had no idea that such competitive teams existed, or what joining a 'squad' would entail, but the idea of representing our hometown at the thing we enjoyed more than anything else seemed too good to be true.

Maybe another case of 'bream as big as dustbin lids', I thought, but a few minutes later we were clambering into the back of Peter's car and on our way to the reservoir, with our minds already set on joining the trial. We also realised that the immediate trip was our chance to practise, before begging to make a return visit in seven days. And thankfully our pleading worked.

On another hot Saturday morning we pulled up on the side of the main road once more and began to unload our gear. It was immediately clear there were many more parked cars than usual, but it wasn't until we walked down the drive to the perimeter path that we saw a horde of teenagers gathered near the water.

There were a similar number of parents watching over them and once we joined the growing throng we also met the handful of adults who ran the Juniors Squad – including a certain Jim Baxter, who would go on to teach me more about the art of match fishing than anyone else. I suppose disclosing that fact is a spoiler for the outcome of the day, but he deserves immediate credit.

Although I didn't catch the most or the biggest fish, Jim and his mates spent ten or fifteen minutes observing each young angler, giving them advice and watching for a while in order to decide what they might be capable of. My turn came after I'd already placed a few small roach in my keepnet, but the bites had agonisingly started to dry up just as Jim approached. He watched me persevere for a few casts before asking to have a look at my rig.

Thanks to Andy's uncle, he was impressed to find me using a size 20 hook tied to a fine hooklength of around two-pound breaking strain, but he still asked if I had anything smaller and lighter. Luckily I had one packet of microscopic, size 24 hooks tied to gossamer-like twelve-ounce nylon, so I was urged to give them a go.

He said I needed to scale everything right down as the sun had risen higher and the faint breeze barely ruffled the surface. He also added an extra shot to the line so my float settled even lower in the water and became a barely visible pimple once I'd recast it to the right spot. I fired out another pouch of maggots with my catapult, which thankfully landed tightly around my float, and a minute later it vanished.

I struck somewhat awkwardly, not used to fishing under any kind of observational pressure, and felt a surge of relief as the rod pulled over against the jagging resistance of a decent fish. Jim cautioned me to take it easy now that I was using such a fine hooklength, showing me how to backwind in order to give a bit of line when necessary. Once I'd eased the roach over the rim of my landing net he smiled and said, "Nice work," before walking away to see the next hopeful contestant.

Thankfully, my brief demonstration had been enough and Andy also managed to do himself justice, so after we'd packed up and re-joined the thirty or so other lads back at the sailing club, our names were amongst those read out. We numbered around fifteen, less than half of those who had turned up in the morning, so we felt rightfully pleased.

We were nowhere near the frame, however, and had to watch on with more than a twinge of envy as three boys were handed small plastic trophies and received enthusiastic applause from the coaches and their fellow competitors. But we were still overjoyed at having been selected to represent our hometown.

Over the next three or four years we took part in a national fishing league that featured different divisions, teams from cities and towns from all over the country and several major events with more than 200 juniors taking part. We had training sessions on rivers like the Nene and Trent, while sometimes meeting in pub function rooms ahead of big matches, where Jim and other fantastic fishermen like Tony Stones and Dave Hodges would help us decide tactics.

The Magic of Fishing

On the odd occasion we were even honoured by a visit from someone in the legendary Barnsley Blacks squad – semi-professional matchmen so skilled and wise that they also fished for England on the international stage. I frequently read about them in my weekly magazines and while my excitement at meeting such 'famous' anglers may sound laughable to a fishermuggle, or even to those who dabble for a bit of relaxation, for me it was a glimpse into an elite world of fishing that I now dreamed of joining.

CHAPTER 12

Pole Position

Thanks to the extra hours of coaching, plus the many new venues, techniques and tips I gained from the Sheffield Juniors squad, my ability to *compete* in fishing matches steadily grew. I even won a few section prizes – beating another fifteen or twenty anglers in one particular stretch of major events held along several miles of river.

Those national competitions were taken seriously by all involved. Everyone was handed a sheet of rules at the draw and when we sometimes fished with the Seniors there were bookmakers on hand, which allowed the more confident or optimistic anglers to have a punt on themselves. Anyone choosing to do so stood the chance of winning a few hundred pounds, in addition to the significant prize money on offer.

It was still fun and completely enjoyable, although my parents, Ben and Granddad began to notice a new era of dedication as I progressed through my early teenage years. Yet one prize remained stubbornly out of reach and it was the one I spent more time dreaming about than any other – that of winning a DWSSC match.

Despite the minor individual successes I'd enjoyed with the Sheffield Juniors, every time I returned to the Trent with my now-familiar club members, the top spot continued to elude me. I managed a few second and third places, which was still a great feeling and meant I went home with a few quid in my pocket, but to get my name engraved on one of the old silver trophies that I watched being handed out at every October prize-giving night, only first would do.

Those coveted trophies continued to evade me until I was sixteen and we arrived at a new stretch of the Trent one cloudless August morning. The talk on the way there had been of how low and clear the river was running and how finicky the fish would be as a result. This would apparently make the draw all the more important because there was a weir at the top end of the stretch, so when I innocently withdrew my hand from the bag with a disk showing number one, I heard several good-natured protests such as "the young'un's only gone and pulled t'flyer!"

I tried to hide my excitement and told Granddad – who had decided I was old enough to fish alone a few years previously – that I was positive it couldn't be *that* good and I was sure he had as much chance of a good day as me. I was given lots of encouragement while we unloaded our tackle and once I'd hauled my gear along twenty or so pegs, losing sight of the coach and most of my fellow anglers, the roar of the weir grew closer.

Eventually I saw the foaming, oxygen-filled water of the pool for myself and at that point I knew I had indeed received a hefty dose of good luck. While the river downstream was low and clear, the churning water in front of me looked so 'fishy' that I felt a bit giddy and muttered to myself, "Bloody 'ell, John, don't blow this."

My pulse was racing and my breathing shallow as I tackled up my Daiwa Porky Pig quivertip rod with a heavy swimfeeder and an extra strong hooklength. Only a keen angler of a certain age will appreciate that reference to a classic rod of its day, but I'd received it for my birthday earlier that year and now believed it had been hiding patiently in my rod bag for this very match.

For younger readers, I'm talking about a workhorse of a fishing rod that was – and still is – capable of launching a three-ounce swimfeeder full of maggots towards the middle of the Trent. And, if you were lucky enough to hook one, it was strong enough to subdue a big chub or indeed anything with serious power that might inhabit the river. It was twice the rod of anything I'd owned before and its smooth cork handle was unblemished, the varnish on its whippings immaculate, and the all-important fluorescent paint on the quivertip glowed orange.

I carefully threaded my line through each eye and willed my fingers to stop trembling, because although I still had forty minutes to prepare and another five hours to fish, it suddenly felt like time was trying to run away from me. I desperately didn't want to end this match like I had so many others – ruing missed opportunities and kicking myself over indecision and wasted time. Not when I'd had such a leg up to begin with.

My fascination with fishing
began at a very early age

Posing with a trout from the
Derwent (using a paper towel!)

Granddad in his element: relaxing by the water's edge with a pipe

Right: My bed at Downing Road, which was in occasional use for nearly four decades and served me well from boy to man

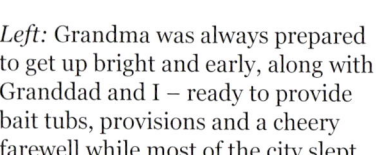

Left: Grandma was always prepared to get up bright and early, along with Granddad and I – ready to provide bait tubs, provisions and a cheery farewell while most of the city slept

Below: My fellow DWSSC club members, during the 1980s, lining up to help empty the coach and reclaim their tackle before another match on the River Trent

Mum and Dad taking a break in their
fruit and veg garden a few years ago

Ben, my first fishing friend, at a local
park pond on another hot afternoon

Jim Baxter, my patient match fishing
mentor, who is still catching plenty
these days

Andy with Peter, his dad, arriving at
the DWSSC clubhouse for a matchday

The lush banks of the River Wey, where I loved exploring after moving to Surrey

This mirror carp, caught in my early thirties, remains my biggest freshwater fish to this day

My friend Steve with a carp caught during our 'wilderness years' of infrequent yet enjoyable fishing trips

Battling a sailfish, which nearly broke three anglers, off the coast of West Africa

Pepe, our guide and friend, holding the giant sailfish before release

The moment of capture: still the most spectacular and beautiful fish I've ever seen in the flesh

My son Fred's first ever catch, a tiny perch from the local canal in Woking

Despite my best efforts, he was more naturally drawn to rugby as a young lad

Lara was and still is one of the more natural anglers amongst the four kids

Left: Andy with an XL carp landed from a commercial match venue

Right: Harry, Andy's son, following in his father's and grandfather's fishing footsteps

Above left: Fraser, the eldest, enjoyed his first trip to a small club pond near Woking

Above right: Ewan wrestling with an eel, caught by his stepdad, during an evening stroll

Right: Rachel, my wife, having a quick cast on the local river

Below: A big Wey chub, caught during the kind of short evening session that I generally enjoy these days

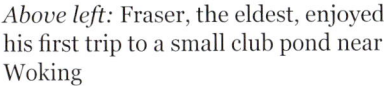

Cherished club friends during the weigh-in at the end of a recent DWSSC match

Simple pleasures: fishing isn't all about catching and is good for both body and mind

Some might smirk at my overblown sense of destiny and drama, but the usual 'knowing feeling' that I'd felt earlier that morning upon waking in my bedroom at Downing Road had been a decade or more in the making. I was now dating girls and trying to get served in pubs, but as I sat down to survey the river's surface and tried to decide where I should try first, I felt more like the awestruck kid who froze when his float first disappeared at The Pond. It was an overwhelming feeling of hope – and of magic.

The sun rose higher and started to blast relentless heat over me as 10am approached. I wiped sweat from my eyes before fumbling the cap off the swimfeeder and carefully pouring in a trickle of bronze maggots from my left palm. I baited the hook with another two of them and looked at my watch again, waiting for the seconds to tick down.

The whistles finally blew and it was time to use the immaculate rod for what it had been designed for – carefully manoeuvring it over my shoulder and lowering the tip behind me, before heaving forward, compressing the carbon blank and letting go of the line with my finger tip at just the right moment to punch the heavy rig far out over the river.

The usual 'splosh' was drowned out by the constant din of the weir and I felt the first twinge of doubt as the current immediately swept everything downstream – the feeder failing to hold position despite the extra lead I'd added. I could feel it bouncing and sliding over gravel, but it eventually found purchase and I placed the rod in its rest, pointed skyward in order to keep most of the line out of the rushing water.

I sat completely still on my seatbox, right hand hovering over the rod handle in anticipation, and scrunched my eyes against the glare. I focused on the curved quivertip that now rocked gently against the flow and wondered if my instincts about the peg would prove justified. But before I had time to lose faith, there was a sudden tap followed by a violent pull. It was a typical bite from a good Trent fish and I connected with something that I knew was no roach or 'skimmer' bream.

I'm not ashamed to admit I grinned like a loon and only just resisted an urge to punch the air like a centre-forward who'd netted a goal within the first minute of a game. Not just because I'd hooked something solid on the first cast – a dream start to any match – but because my confidence in the peg had proven correct. It had taken only sixty seconds for a decent fish to find two tiny maggots out there in the vast expanse of boiling water, which told me something: the swim must be *stuffed*.

After a tense battle, I eventually guided a glistening chub of about three pounds into my landing net, which was a great catch at any stage of a match on the Trent. There were very few mobiles in those days and smart phones were yet to be invented, but if they had been I'm sure I would have paused to take a picture and text Granddad the good news before recasting. I was so happy that I actually considered running down to see him, just to tell him this really was my big chance.

I wanted to tell the whole world, but I knew I needed to stay focused if I was to make the most of my draw. So that's what I did, and it wasn't until two and a half hours had passed, halfway through the match, when serious doubts started to creep in. I'd caught a few more, smaller chub, but I'd struggled to cast my feeder to the same spot with enough consistency and the bites were now taking longer to materialise, or sometimes they weren't coming at all.

I knew I'd had a good start, but it began to feel like I could be wasting this marvellous peg. Either that or it wasn't quite as good as it had initially seemed. I feverishly went over my options and tried a few standard adjustments, like a lighter and longer hooklength and different bait combinations, but in the end it was another dose of serendipity that saved the day.

I'd just refilled the swimfeeder and opened the bail arm on my reel, before swinging the rig out in front of me to prepare for another cast, when the line slipped from my finger and everything plummeted into the river below my feet. Being just downstream from the big weir, the bank had been strengthened by several long sheets of corrugated metal that were staked in place to help resist the erosive current, so rather than the riverbed sloping gently away from the shoreline, there must have been at least three feet of water.

I swore at what seemed like another example of me beginning to mess things up and re-engaged my reel, ready to go through preparations again, when something unexpected happened. As I started to wind in, turning the handle rapidly in frustration, I suddenly felt a jagging resistance and realised there was a fish on. I was gobsmacked, as the bait had only been in the water for a few seconds, but I wasn't about to complain.

It was a chunky perch of about half a pound, which fought admirably and lifted my spirits even if I hadn't caught it by design. The bonus fish soon joined the small gang of chub already in my keepnet and at that point I nearly made a silly mistake – I almost dismissed it as a fluke and prepared to cast back to the usual spot. Thankfully, just before I did, a spark of reason flashed across a synapse somewhere in my brain and I wondered if there might be anything else to be caught down there.

I lowered my rod and gently swung the rig out almost directly below me, this time on purpose, reasoning that I should give it a few minutes, just in case. But it took even less time than that for the tip to flicker and then pull down more firmly. I struck and shook my head in disbelief as another decent fish fought for freedom.

A second 'stripey' shook its head angrily and rushed about in the current for a while before I got the upper hand – and only then did I speculate there could be a whole *shoal* of fish down there. In which case, I realised, it would mean I'd been ignorantly casting over them for more than half of the match. And that did indeed prove to be the case but, thankfully, it wasn't too late to make amends.

During the next hour or so, my accidental discovery of an angling goldmine had me offering numerous mental thank-yous to the fishing gods, who must surely have been on my side. I landed perch after perch, enjoying some of the best action I've ever experienced on a natural venue, and once again started to believe I could win the match.

It made for a beautiful high and the only concerns still niggling at my newfound joy were the usual question of how everyone else was doing and, as the final hour approached, whether I would have enough bait. I was getting through far more than normal as I tried to keep the hungry fish preoccupied, ensuring they wouldn't get spooked by the commotion each time one of them slipped up.

Granddad always kept faith in his old metal bait tin that could hold two pint of maggots at most, but by then I'd realised how important regular and sometimes heavy feeding could be on the Trent. I saved my paper round earnings before each trip and usually went armed with half a gallon of maggots in a plastic bait bucket, especially if the stretch was known to be in good form, so I couldn't believe I was down to a handful, with a full sixty minutes remaining.

I grew paranoid that everyone else might be having a red-letter day too, or at least the men who were immediately downstream from me and therefore also near the weir. I really didn't want to stop catching, but with my bait bucket almost empty and forty minutes still to go, I knew my best bet was to visit Granddad, who was halfway down the field, and see if he had any spare. I reasoned this would also allow me to assess how others were doing, so left my rod and set off at a trot.

I was sweating heavily by the time I jogged up to him and he was surprised to see me. He listened with a faint smile as I breathlessly explained how my peg really *was* a flyer; how I'd been catching non-stop for the last two hours; and how I thought I could actually win the match. A typically thrifty Yorkshireman, he couldn't believe I'd got through so much bait, but without a selfish bone in his body he gladly let me have the rest of his.

He kept a few back for his hook, explaining he'd not had much luck anyway and repeatedly reassured me that he didn't need the rest. I felt momentarily torn, half wanting to stay with him to demonstrate that I hadn't become completely obsessed by winning, but also knowing that every minute I dawdled by his side might mean one less perch in the net.

None of those I'd called out to as I'd gone past them said they were "doin' owt," but I still feared the unknown situation past Granddad's peg, so it's probably fair to say I *was* obsessed with this golden opportunity to claim my first DWSSC victory. And thankfully it was Granddad who gave me licence to leave.

"Well you'd better get back to it, John, and make sure you win," he said with a wink, and with that I was racing back along the bank, wishing Grandma had put more than one small bottle of lemonade in my packed lunch but eager to see if I could use the fresh supply of maggots to make the most of the final twenty minutes.

I arrived back to my seatbox and hastily filled the feeder, smiling at the fact these maggots weren't a uniform bronze colour like mine, but the multi-coloured mix that I'd grown up with and which Granddad still preferred. Despite the ticking clock, I was reminded of a day we'd been fishing on the Trent at Marnham, a tidal stretch where we sometimes stayed in the caravan.

During one of those long weekends I'd caught a lot more fish than Granddad by casting a swimfeeder towards the middle of the river, just as I'd been doing at the start of this match, while he'd been content to watch his usual – and now old-fashioned – perch bobber as it swayed next to a big clump of weeds for hours on end.

He had no interest in the technical innovations sweeping through the sport and his only investment beyond the 1970s was a cheap telescopic rod that he could collapse down and stow in his wicker basket, meaning he didn't have to carry a heavy rod bag anymore. He was content to lay that new rod on the bank or borrow a rest from me, knowing that I always carried a landing net for the rare occasions he required one too.

As I thought back to that particular day at Marnham, I remembered landing yet another small bream and feeling a prick of shame, rather than pride, as I held it up for my idol to see. Not because he cared much whether he was catching or not, but simply because he was the one who started my fishing odyssey and I wanted him to have as much success as I was now enjoying.

I didn't mean to brag each time I showed him another fish, but later that day I realised that he didn't need my

The Magic of Fishing

sympathy and was still perfectly capable of success. His float had eventually registered some interest late in the afternoon and as it sank out of sight he struck into something much more powerful than I had managed to entice with my carbon rod, bucket of maggots and chemically etched hooks.

I strode over to watch the ensuing battle and winced on several occasions when it seemed the fish must surely snap his line, or momentarily became snagged in the weeds where it had been lurking. It was a proper battle of nerves, but his skill prevailed and the fish finally surfaced. I saw a red tail first, vibrant against the murky water, before a broad back loomed into sight. Then, as its energy waned, the fish slowly tilted over in the current – revealing an impossibly deep, tiger-like flank.

We both gasped as the biggest perch we had ever seen rested on the surface for a moment, before flaring its spiky, almost prehistoric-looking dorsal fin and kicking away in a last attempt to evade capture. The final minute of the fight was even more fraught as neither of us could bear the thought of losing it, but Granddad managed to keep his composure and I was there to help with the net.

We had no scales or camera with us but confidently estimated it was around three pounds in weight, which is a true 'specimen' perch even today. And I would have gladly swapped all of my skimmers, roach and gudgeon for that one fish. We were both speechless, but I didn't need to say anything as he could tell I was impressed by the look on my face. And not only by the size of that incredible fish, but by the wisdom and humility he'd demonstrated in waiting all day to catch it.

I recalled that as soon as I'd got back to my basket, I'd set up my own float rod and tried to mimic his tactics, but I didn't have a clump of weeds nearby, or indeed his patience, so it didn't pay off. Yet his simple approach and the reward he got for it had taught me another valuable lesson in keeping an open mind. I had been feeling concerned for my mentor most of the day, but as we packed up it was replaced by admiration.

So as I prepared to start fishing below the weir again, towards the end of that momentous August match, I nicked one red, one yellow and one white maggot onto my hook, remembering Granddad's words as he slipped his monster perch back into the river a few years earlier: "Do you know, John, I thought there might be a big'un hiding in those weeds, so I tried a big bunch of different coloured maggots and it obviously couldn't resist them."

When the shrill whistles blew at 3pm I felt satisfied that I'd done everything possible to stand a chance of winning, and therefore couldn't stop humming to myself as I slowly packed away my gear and then sat gazing down at the miraculous marginal run that had been so generous to me. If there was a trace of regret, it was only that the perch had still been queuing up to attack my bait right until the end.

I felt sure I could have kept catching them all evening, but as I tried to get the last few drops of lemonade into my parched mouth, I wasn't about to complain. I waited impatiently for the weigh-in, which traditionally commenced at the furthest peg from the coach – in this case, mine. It was quite some time until the first two men arrived and they looked as hot and sweaty as I felt. One had bronzed and leathery skin while another had a shiny, pink face that seemed less familiar with the great outdoors.

"'As tha' done alreet, kid?" they inquired and I nodded in an exaggerated fashion, knowing I'd put more fish in my net than on any other match I'd fished. Yet it was only when I came to lift my keepnet from the water that I realised just how special the day had been. I struggled to move the lower section above the surface and the water began to explode as twenty or thirty good fish protested at leaving the water again. It looked like a miniature trawler net about to come aboard a boat and the weary men behind me started to jabber in excitement.

"Bloody 'ell, John, what's tha' got in there?" one of them asked, while another exclaimed, "Chuffin' 'ell, he's caned 'em!" They joined me to help haul the catch up the bank and I would have struggled without them. I'd never seen so many fish together, never mind in my net, and received a barrage of questions about where I'd located them, what bait I'd used and how the hell I'd caught so many.

I was in my element and tried to answer all of them, talking and watching as they carefully transferred the fish into the weigh net before heaving it towards old John Swift, who had now joined us with the scales. Once the net was securely hooked in place they let go and John's beefy arms visibly shook as everyone crowded closer to see how far round the needle would leap.

"Tha's got over nineteen pounds there!" one of them shouted. "Ruddy 'ell," said another. And John beamed at me as one of his friends relieved him of the burden and carried it to the river's edge. As they strained to lower the weigh net below the bank and into the water, I glanced up and nearly jumped for joy to see Granddad had arrived, just in time to see them go.

He gawped at the torrent of fish being released back into the river while Mr Swift announced my weight as nineteen pounds and seven ounces, before jotting it down next to my name and peg number – which was one of course. Granddad shook my hand and said he'd never seen anything like it before. Indeed, no one in the club had. In the 1980s, if you landed on a big shoal of decent bream and had enough bait, it was possible to land well over fifty pounds of fish, but catching nearly twenty pounds of perch and chub was a great result by any standards.

Nowadays, the angling news is full of mind-boggling match reports from heavily stocked commercial fisheries, usually made up of countless carp which are now as numerous in many of our manmade lakes as those perch were under my feet on the Trent. I myself have broken the old 'ton' (100 pounds) barrier a few times in recent years, but it's not unheard of for winners of major commercial matches to require ten keepnets and register hauls of 400 pounds or more.

Some, including myself at times, view that kind of feat as bordering on ridiculous, even if there's undoubtedly a different kind of skill required to catch more than the rest in such events. But on that scorching August afternoon so many years ago, a double-figure catch from the Trent was something of a field day for the modest angling ambitions of the Dronfield Woodhouse Sports and Social Club. My nineteen pounds, seven ounces was heralded as the winning weight before anyone else's keepnet had even been assessed, finally allowing me to believe I'd done it.

The jinx was seemingly broken and I couldn't stop smiling. I let the knowledge sink in as the small but growing group of anglers moved on to see what had happened in peg number two. I heaved my rod bag and basket straps over my shoulders, grabbed my sodden keepnet and set off after them, keen to see what my neighbour had managed. After all, I thought, he was only a little further downstream from the weir's oxygenating cascade and perhaps he'd found a similar shoal of fish.

I therefore felt relief, but also a touch of guilt when I saw the elderly man had actually struggled and only managed a few small ones. "'E's 'ad what?" he gasped when the others told him of my achievement, just a short stroll along the bank, yet there was no hint of resentment – just the second of many handshakes I received on our sweltering migration back to the coach.

There was an ice cream van in the carpark and it materialised gradually, like a mirage, as we walked the last few pegs. Seeing it there waiting for us was the cherry on the cake, after a final weigh-in confirmed beyond doubt that I was a winner. No one else had come close to double figures and I could barely contain my pride, but I did my best to accept all the congratulations with the same modesty as those who'd gone before me.

A Mr Whippie with a Flake felt like the perfect way to celebrate the long-awaited victory, and I was still finishing it when old John Swift stood up in the coach, ready to formally announce the results. Many of the men had watched me persevere over the years and knew how much the win meant to me, so it may have been my heightened emotional state but I'm sure I received a much louder round of applause than usual.

CHAPTER 13

Flying South

As 1999 drew to a close, I celebrated in the middle of Sheffield, joining my mates and thousands of other happy, drunken revellers who bounced up and down for hours as music thumped from huge sound systems. Before midnight arrived, we all gazed skywards as fireworks exploded for the best part of half an hour, building in intensity until they filled my entire field of vision.

I no longer lived in the city and was only back for the Christmas break, so it was a night of looking forward and celebrating the arrival of a new year, decade, century and millennium – but also of thinking back and contemplating how much had happened, and changed, over a relatively short space of time.

Four years earlier I'd graduated from university with a quirky degree in film studies, but hadn't had a clue what to do with it. And a year after that I'd been working in a busy call centre for nearly 12 months when Ben asked me to be his best man at his wedding in Texas. Sensing not just a chance to do a good deed, but also to end my weekday routine of trying to resolve never-ending complaints, I naturally accepted.

He had fallen for Erica during his studies in North Carolina, after his tennis skills had taken him across the Atlantic to take up a sports scholarship. Now he'd decided to stay in the States, planning to tie the knot at a sprawling ranch near San Antonio that summer. The impressive property was owned by Erica's uncle and was grand enough to have hosted several members of the Bush family, including the former president, but it would also be my home for a week before the big day.

I remember there was a small lake that held some largemouth bass, an American species of fish I'd never seen until then, but I soon came to love spending the odd hour trying to catch them with floating lures. They sometimes followed my imitation prey and then engulfed it with heart-stopping aggression, which only added to the special memories of that trip.

I also enjoyed some incredible hospitality, as did my friend Emma, who was there on bridesmaid duty. In fact we enjoyed ourselves so much that, by the time we left, we had become more than just good friends.

After returning to Sheffield and a more sedate pace of life, I had a brief spell on the dole before falling into a career in public relations, or 'PR' as it's often known. It really did happen by accident, too – thanks to a peculiar chain of events that began when I found a friend crying at a party one night. I thought she'd perhaps had one drink too many, but that wasn't entirely the case, as she explained how she worked for a PR agency and was in trouble because she was meant to have rewritten a company's promotional brochure by Monday morning.

She hadn't even made a start and wasn't in the right frame of mind to do so now, so what was she – or indeed I – supposed to do? Despite having consumed quite a few cans of beer myself, I offered to have a stab at some words that I felt better conveyed the firm's messages to potential customers. This only took me an hour and, after handing her a few sheets of scribbles around midnight, I thought nothing more of it until the following week.

That's when I received a sheepish phone call from my friend and she explained how, after she'd typed up and presented the work on Monday morning, the agency's owner had been so impressed that it eventually led to an embarrassing confession. To my amazement, she'd admitted the work wasn't entirely her own and, rather than reprimanding her, her boss had asked to meet the mystery writer.

My unorthodox approach to job-hunting had nothing to do with fishing, of course, but the opportunity I unwittingly created would come to influence my angling experiences in all kinds of unexpected ways over the coming years. Just six months after joining my friend at the small firm, I found myself unemployed again. We unfortunately lost a major client and both of us were out on our ears with no notice – yet in that time I'd decided PR was the thing for me.

After sending out numerous letters, I was soon picking up my new profession at another of Sheffield's communications companies, where I enjoyed eighteen fun-filled months and learned plenty of useful things from a former newspaper editor. I liked my new boss and had also bought a small, terraced house with Emma, which was located near the office, so everything seemed rosy for quite some time.

However, after spotting it one evening in *The Star*,

The Magic of Fishing

nothing could stop me applying for the position of 'press officer' at a company called Yorkshire Cable – the main reason being a crucial line in the advert, which stated the successful applicant would receive excellent benefits including a company car. And a car, I reasoned, would enable me to drive to any fishing destination I fancied.

I got the job and although still based in Sheffield I also got to drive a lot – proudly travelling to Bradford once a week, or even more exotic places like Slough on occasion, in a brand-new Ford Fiesta. Yet despite the early momentum in my burgeoning career, around eight months later I found myself being made redundant for a second time.

My employer had merged with another cable company and the powers-that-be decided the press team, along with many other departments, needed 'rationalising'. All Yorkshire-based PR roles were to be scrapped which, alongside the painful break-up of my relationship with Emma, seemed like the starting pistol for doom and depression. And so it proved, because depressed was exactly how I felt during the month-long consultation period.

I was down and out until my last day in the office or, to be more specific, the point when I entered a glass cubicle to take a call from head office. I was due to leave the company a few hours later, but the person calling was none other than the director of communications. After commiserating with me for the situation I found myself in, he said I'd impressed him during the short time we'd worked together and, if I wanted it, there was a job waiting for me at the newly formed company's headquarters in Surrey.

I'd never heard of Woking, the town where the HQ was now established, but over the next few days I was offered a staggering pay rise (which, little did I know, the increased cost of living would make almost irrelevant) and six months to make up my mind. He also offered to put me up in various hotels and pubs during the trial period, which would let me make the big decision after spending some proper time down there, but also meant tedious drives up and down the M1 every week.

I took the plunge and entered the frenetic world of corporate communications in the south-east, all while wrestling with the idea of leaving my family and friends on a more permanent basis. It was March when I bit the bullet by putting my house in Sheffield up for let and, once I'd found some tenants, I started to receive about half the monthly rent I would soon be paying for a one-bedroom flat in Surrey.

My ever-supportive and long-suffering parents drove me down to Woking on moving day, helping me shift my few possessions, including my seatbox, rod bag and nets, into the poky, ground-floor bedsit. I squeezed them under or around the small dining table in my new home because there wasn't anywhere else to put them, but then I had no local friends to invite round for a meal anyway.

Despite the initial thrill of working in a head office and learning how an even larger company was run, my first few months down there were some of the loneliest in my life. I often had no one to see and nowhere to go after the long working days ended, or at least not without a train trip into London to have a few extortionately priced pints with old mates.

I therefore started to believe the gamble I'd taken was good for my CV but not for my soul – feeling increasingly confident that I'd be back up north once I'd done my time and could start hunting for a senior position in Sheffield. That would surely be within reach,

I reasoned, now I'd encountered national newspaper journalists, slick Soho PR agencies and charismatic company directors with degrees from Oxford or Cambridge.

As June and the end of my trial period rolled around, my mind was still set. Right until the moment I came across an advertisement for Woking and District Angling Association while flicking through a local paper. Only then did I stop to consider if there might be something more for me there. And after finding the determination needed to contact them, I happily paid the modest joining fee and my first year's subscription, before they sent me a membership book containing several hand-drawn maps of their waters.

One sketch depicted a cluster of four lakes in a nearby village called Send, while others detailed mile upon mile of the River Wey that I could apparently now access through a variety of farm gates, churchyards and woodland paths. I had found something to feel truly happy about again and, with the new season still over a fortnight away, I spent the next two weekends driving around and exploring every inch of the maps on foot.

It was the beginning of what would become one of the hottest summers on record and after each 'reccy' concluded I returned to the suffocating heat of my flat and tried to get some sleep. It was no mean feat for a northern lad, particularly with the screech of trains running past the block every ten minutes, cutting through the whir of an expensive-yet-ineffective 'air-cooling' unit at the end of my single bed, but it wasn't just the noise and temperature that made me restless. It was a growing feeling of excitement about all the wondrous new places to fish I'd just discovered.

I've always enjoyed my own company, but climbing stiles and stumbling across wild meadows to find the meandering river – glistening in the sun as it gurgled gently under a bridge, or around a bend and into a dark wood – were some of the best solo adventures I can recall. Some people set out to conquer mountains or navigate oceans in order to achieve fulfilment, but I was utterly content to spend my weekends driving along winding lanes blooming with early summer colour, scouting for new waters and the fish they might hold.

I stopped and asked farmers for directions to a pub, church or manor house I'd circled on the map, drive a bit further and then slow the car to a crawl as the entrance to another interesting spot approached, always hoping to discover somewhere else packed with potential. And I savoured all the differences between this new landscape and the more familiar Peak District I'd left behind, because this new, gentler county was starting to feel like home.

After the long, dark winter months, the pressure of starting a new job and week after week of moving from one strange bed to another, I suddenly felt I belonged there – or at least for a while. I could finally put down some tentative roots and, with the 16th of June just days away, I also discovered the local tackle shop. It was only a short walk from the office and quickly became a tempting lunchtime distraction whenever I could afford the time.

Unfortunately, and like so many other tackle dens I knew as a younger man, Goldsworth Angling no longer exists, but that special shop served me well during the next phase of my fishing life. The men behind the counter initially frowned or smirked when I asked for "two pints o' casters," with a flat A. Then came gentle jokes from the owner and his able assistant, 'Sharkey', as they got to know me better. And by the end of my first season in Woking, they greeted me warmly with a shout of "It's Sheffield John!" every time I tinkled the bell.

I often loitered there, swapping endless stories and debating where I had the best chance of catching various species of fish in my new piscatorial playground. They were initially surprised by the frequency of my visits and during that first summer I used almost every lunch break to stock up for the coming weekend – such was the luxury lifestyle of a single man in his twenties who was now earning enough money to cover rent, bills and frequent tackle shop binges.

My social life eventually took off too and I sometimes swapped Friday night fishing for a game of tennis with a new mate, Nick Rawlings, drunken pub quizzes with my neighbour, Simon, or post-work drinks with my boss and the rest of the PR team. Yet angling was rapidly becoming an all-consuming passion once more. My cramped flat filled up with even more rods, bags, books and maps, while wet nets were regularly left to dry outside my front door. I was back in my element and felt alive again.

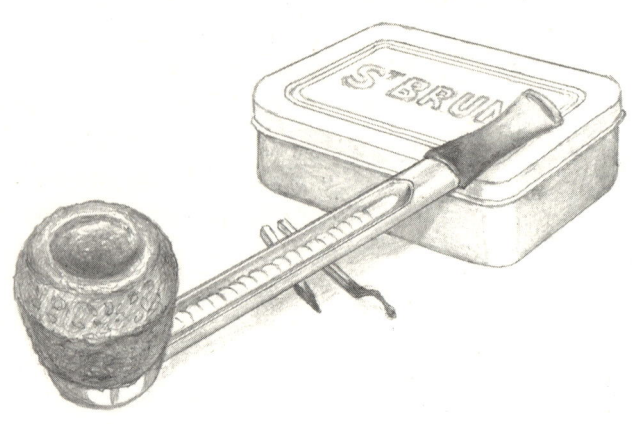

CHAPTER 14

Change

The boom in manmade, heavily stocked fisheries, or 'commercials' as they're known, began a little too late for Granddad – although he would have hated the cost of day tickets and struggled to comprehend the concept of catching more carp in a morning than he'd landed in his entire life.

I doubt he would have understood sixteen-metre carbon poles costing thousands of pounds, barrows loaded with sophisticated tackle or self-hooking 'method' rigs either, but he would have appreciated the secure car parks, well-made paths and the level banks. Indeed, those convenient angling hotspots which proved such a catalyst for change may have extended his fishing career if he hadn't already lost interest by the time anything decent materialised around Sheffield.

The first digger-gouged ponds were often derided as 'muddy puddles', being rather featureless and uninspiring for the first few years, but they slowly matured and began to dominate the pleasure and match fishing scenes thanks to the extra comfort, security and guaranteed bites they afforded. This recipe for good fishing and good business soon appealed to DWSSC too, which meant the years of our coach trips to the Trent were sadly but understandably drawing to an end.

Many of the members were just too old for the long walks, unpredictable pegs and – particularly towards the end of the 1990s – dwindling fish stocks. Blame for the river's decline was placed on inland cormorants, the changing nature of the power stations, farmers' fertiliser and any number of other theories. Ironically, some said it was down to the river becoming *cleaner* but, whatever the truth, it was undeniable that some of our final Trent matches were a total washout.

Well into his eighties, and having already beaten cancer, Granddad was rapidly losing his strength too. It was a struggle to get him to the pub on a Saturday morning whenever I was back in Sheffield for a weekend, and fishing of any kind was off the cards, but I still phoned Grandma whenever I could and told her to get him dressed for 11am. Then I'd drive over and take him to the pub and the bookies, before returning for lunch.

She loved receiving those calls because it was increasingly hard for her to raise his spirits and get him motivated to go outside, but our occasional Saturday trips always seemed to reignite the remaining embers of his enthusiasm. For a short while, at least, the sparkle returned to his eyes and he felt like a younger man again – back in the familiar environments he'd known all his life.

His heart was failing, his knees weakening and his back seizing up, but his mind was still pretty sharp, if a little cynical and weary. "Don't get old, John," he advised me whenever we sat down with a pint of Trophy in our usual seats near the pool table. "I won't," I'd reply, secretly hoping my regular promises didn't mean I was now destined to die young.

He still knew most of the regulars for a quick exchange and he usually managed to play a game of pool with me, but it took all of his remaining energy in the last couple of years. He could still demonstrate some skill too, but sometimes preferred to remain seated, studying the racing pages or asking me about my life down south. He would often urge me to 'sow my wild oats' and if anything was troubling me at work, or indeed elsewhere, he would listen quietly before saying, "Aye, but worse things 'appen at sea."

One drizzly, autumnal Saturday morning, he struggled to make it from the car to the pub. Once seated and having caught his breath, he leant over the table and fixed me with his pale blue eyes. "Look after her for me, won't you, John?" he said.

Shocked, I bluffed cheeriness and pretended not to understand what he meant, but it was naïve and callous of me. It forced him to clarify what he'd just tried to say and restate it in a more dramatic way. Sighing, he said, "I'm dying, lad," before smiling weakly and shaking his head as I began to protest.

I eventually shut my mouth and he went on, "I've not long for this world and I'm tired of living, so look after Grandma when I've gone." Then he paused, before adding, "Promise me." And of course I *did* promise him, although I hoped he still had a few years left in him yet – and told him so. He smiled more broadly. "I've had a good life," he said, before telling me to "sup up" and help him to the bookies next door.

I can't remember if it was a few months or even a year after he'd spoken those sombre words to me, but I'll never forget the call I received one evening while sitting alone in my flat in Woking, watching TV and thinking about a work problem or some other mundane concern. The landline rang unexpectedly at around 9pm and made me jump. I answered and heard Dad's voice.

He was being strong and calm as ever, but explained that he was with Granddad, and a nurse, in the front room at Downing Road. Grandma was somewhere close by, too, but he suggested I should speak to Granddad myself, because he was now close to the end and being cared for around the clock.

I felt like I was suffocating as the phone went quiet and I waited to hear someone speak, or indeed to hear *any* noise. I desperately willed Granddad to sound normal – happy, confident and charismatic, as he had for most of my life – but what I eventually heard was a barely discernible whisper. A strained version of my granddad's voice struggled to say, "Hello John, how y'doing?" with a deep tiredness that belayed his condition.

I felt angry and ashamed but I couldn't think of anything meaningful to say back; other than "Hello," and "how are you feeling?" I knew damn well how he was feeling, but I didn't want to believe it, so we had a brief chat about nothing in particular and I told him I loved him, before Dad was back on the other end.

He moved as far away from the sofa as the fixed telephone cord would allow him and quietly explained that he was going to stay overnight. His dad might not make it through and I should expect an update soon.

The dreaded news came the next day, when I received another call from Dad to confirm Granddad had passed earlier that morning. He mentioned the nurse was married to a fisherman and she'd apparently distracted Granddad with simple anecdotes about her husband whenever he became a bit distressed. Right at the end, he'd had his wife, his son, a caring nurse and a few more dreams of big fish.

I felt terrible that I was miles away, just as I had been when my dear Aunty May had died during my time at university, and even when we'd lost our much-loved family dog. I had only recently moved to Surrey when Meg, our golden retriever, was put down due to terrible arthritis. She was only nine and I'd spent many hours of my teenage years with her, walking across wild moorland or following the course of streams while she balanced ridiculously large branches in her mouth.

There was some solace in the fact that, much like Aunty May and good old Meg, Granddad had been loved and looked after right until his final breath. He'd even sensed his end was coming, so it couldn't be deemed a shock either. I tried to keep remembering how he'd said, "I've had a good life," not long before I last saw him – and it *was* a good life. One I felt lucky to have shared for nearly three decades.

I didn't cry until a week later, after I'd driven up to Sheffield for the funeral and to be with my family. Even after the usual slog round the M25 and up the M1, I didn't stay much longer than half an hour once I'd arrived, soon heading over to Grandma's house to bring her back to Mum and Dad's. It was the least I could do to help and, on the way over, I became conscious it was the first time I'd driven to Downing Road knowing that Granddad wouldn't be there.

Even when he was in hospital, being treated for cancer, I'd been too young to really appreciate what was going on, but this time there was no denying he wouldn't be smiling at me from one of their worn leather chairs. Nor would he be having a wash in the kitchen sink, cleaning his pipe out with a penknife, or strolling in his back garden with his big hands clasped behind his back.

Grandma was still there, though, and she seemed so alone in the silent home where they'd spent so many happy years together. She was putting on a brave face and only after she'd fussed with her hair, checked for her keys at least three times and found her reading glasses could we leave the house. I was glad to get her outside and into the fresh night air, where the world still felt partially real.

We approached my car, which was the first one I'd bought for myself, and, as I helped her into the passenger seat, I recalled how Granddad had given me his old Austin Maestro a few years before that, which was the first car I'd called my own. All too briefly, though, because while it served me well, including on a nervy road trip to France with Emma, some bloody joyriders had stolen it before leaving a burned-out shell up at the local reservoirs.

I flinched at the memory, before turning the ignition and heading back to my childhood home. Only once we were halfway there did we make faltering, clumsy attempts to say something, before succumbing to overwhelming grief. We simultaneously dropped any remaining defences and the floodgates opened, unashamedly and unstoppably. We wailed and moaned and choked our way through the last couple of miles, still sobbing loudly and gasping for air when I pulled into Dad's driveway.

We sat helplessly for a few minutes longer before lurching into a hug – holding onto each other tightly until the tears slowly abated. Finally, we pulled apart, blowing our noses and wiping at red-rimmed eyes, before mercifully making our way into the warmth and love of the house.

It would be a few more years until I could visit Grandma without more tears stinging her tired eyes at some point during the evening, but I kept my promise to help look after her in the best way I could. And now I was living nearly 180 miles away, that meant continuing my long tradition of driving north every month throughout the summer and staying with her the night before each matchday.

It was a small contribution to the rest of my family's outstanding care and dedication, but I knew she looked forward to those visits – when one of her adult grandchildren would once more stay with her overnight, much like they had done twenty or thirty years earlier. Nothing really changed about my sleepovers either. Granddad was no longer there, of course, but I still ate the same food she liked to prepare in the same dinky kitchen and I still stored my tackle overnight in the garage.

We still chatted late into the evenings and she would usually offer me a couple of bottles of beer. Sometimes I even persuaded her to have a Bailey's with me, which she eventually developed a particular fondness for. And the peak of our Friday night ritual was the local weather forecast following the news, when we'd both fall silent and hear my meteorological fate for the following day.

Thanks to the advent of the internet, I usually had a good idea of what to expect already, but it was still an important part of our shared preparations, offering an opportunity to discuss whether I would need lots of sun cream, shades and a cap, or waterproofs and a fishing umbrella. If a forecast seemed really bleak it would always send her into a fit of worry – rummaging around upstairs to find a musty overcoat of Granddad's, despite the fact I had a Gore-Tex jacket in the car.

She still insisted on making my packed lunches well into her eighties and I even slept in the same single bed. Its legs and springs were starting to collapse by then and everything would suddenly slant over if I rolled too close to the edge. My feet also stuck out at the end, but I didn't care because I could still gaze up at the familiar polystyrene ceiling while pulling up the same, worn-down blankets I'd known as a kid.

Those crumbling white tiles had been my canvas for countless hopeful dreams over the years and it always felt special to be back in the spare room, even in my thirties. I wished Granddad could somehow join me on one more match and, despite my general atheism, often imagined him looking down on me from somewhere – wishing me 'tight lines' for the morning. I never escaped that tinge of sadness and knew that some things had changed forever but, as I began to drift towards sleep, I still felt a familiar tingle of magic.

CHAPTER 15

Carp Fever

The lily-studded pools and picturesque lakes owned by Woking and District Angling Association felt a million miles from the rocky shoreline of Damflask, or the graffiti-covered, needle-strewn (at the time) concrete surroundings of Sheffield Canal. They were mellow places, matching the romantic descriptions of more famous southern venues I'd read about in angling books, so it didn't take long for me to become infatuated with the pursuit of their enigmatic residents.

Even when I was reunited with Emma and we moved to the nearby village of Ripley, before getting married, the lure of trying to catch those cunning carp, some of them weighing over forty pounds, became quite addictive. I acquired a canvas bivvie, so I could occasionally stay at the lakes overnight, plus a folding bed, electronic bite alarms, two powerful carbon rods and matching Shimano reels.

It was expensive gear but allowed me to set my carefully planned traps on a Friday evening and spend occasional weekends living and sleeping outside, just waiting for one of those wily fish to slip up. And if they did, they usually rushed off wildly – taking line at a furious rate and making my alarm and reel screech out in unison. It was a new, exciting and strategic way to fish, which had me thinking about the next trip with the close of each session on the bank.

I also became fascinated with the multitude of different colours, textures and flavours of boilies on offer. These highly nutritious and scientific baits were – and still are – made from secret ingredients, bound together with eggs and then rolled into small balls of paste, before being boiled for a minute or two. One might say a modern version of Granddad's paste recipe, but featuring anything from 'pre-digested enzymes' to green lipped muscle extract and essential citrus oils.

Nowadays the freezers and shelves of most tackle shops groan under the weight of bags of boilies but, back then, they were still a relatively new innovation. Their tough outer skin deterred the attentions of smaller fish during many hours in the water, while allowing natural compounds and chemical flavours to leach out and attract the carp.

I spent many happy days testing red salmon and cranberry flavour, the fishy Trigga brand or mouth-watering Maple-8 baits and, much like the vanilla or honey-scented paste of my youth, I'm sure some of the allure was in my mind, as much as any preference the fish might have. However, it's fair to say boilies changed the face of specimen fishing and indeed the size of many species of fish living in our waters. The regular use of high-protein baits, including hard pellets that were originally designed to feed stock fish, has seen the record weights of many UK freshwater species jump several times in the last decade or two.

The way these modern baits were presented – the clever ruses and technical thinking behind the modern rigs designed to trick the most cautious of giants – also took carp fishing to a different level. I've since lost touch with the specimen scene, only reading about or watching the fantastic achievements of dedicated big fish anglers from a distance, but the pinnacle of my modest exploits occurred a long time ago, during a late-spring evening session after work.

I arrived at the car park of WDAA's largest lake at around 7pm and heaved my gear down to the furthest, narrow end of the triangular water. I set up opposite some low-hanging trees on the far bank and planned to fish for a couple hours, until dusk. I wasn't really expecting to catch anything in such a short space of time, but it was a chance to unwind and put some bait into a swim I was priming for later in the summer.

It began to feel like a memorable session almost immediately, however, with the rare sight and sound of giant stag beetles taking to the air all around me. There was only one other fisherman on the complex too. I soaked up the peace before firing a few boilies at a curtain of fresh green leaves that trailed in the water opposite. Then I then took my time over casting – carefully landing both rigs within a foot or two of the natural cover.

Once the rods were in their rests and the line was in the buzzers, I sat back in my chair and watched bats skimming the surface as the light began to fade. I still didn't feel particularly expectant, but an hour later one of the bite alarms flared into life, making me jump with its constant tone as something big made a rush up the lake to my right.

I'd caught carp up to about eighteen pounds the year before, so after lifting the rod I immediately knew it might be something a bit special. Tightening the drag further, I tried to slow the initial run, but it showed no sign of stopping. The fish stripped thirty yards of line in no time and I had to plunge the rod tip under the surface and hold on for dear life, wincing as the line began to veer towards a tangle of submerged branches on my own bank.

The fish charged even further away and the taut nylon began to send back worrying sensations as it tripped over submerged branches and roots under maximum strain. Just as I feared there was little chance of ever seeing the runaway beast, the constant pressure finally began to tell and the searing dash ground to a halt. The distant fish resisted my attempts to regain line for some minutes further, boring deep and then stubbornly sulking somewhere out in the middle of the lake, which only built up my hopes that this must be one of the 'biggies'.

Beads of sweat pricked my forehead as I tried to coax the carp towards me with trembling arms. It was the most dramatic tussle I'd had with a freshwater fish and a good fifteen minutes passed before it was back near my feet and ploughing doggedly up and down the margin. And when it eventually succumbed, rolling briefly on the surface, I glimpsed a staggering, pale flank – swearing out loud, because it also appeared to be the biggest fish I'd ever played.

I tried to steady myself as I groped about for the landing net handle in the gloom, eventually finding it before nervously guiding a magnificent mirror carp over the cord. Once I'd thrown my rod to one side and knelt to grab both sides of the frame, I hoisted gently upwards and stared down at the majestic fish in disbelief. I immediately guessed it must be well over the twenty-pound mark, despite the fact I'd never landed a 'twenty' before, but also wondered if it could be bigger still.

Therefore, before I dared lift my catch from the water, I decided I needed the help and reassurance of a witness. I left my captive wallowing in the edge, securely contained within the large net, and raced down the bank to see if my fellow club member was still fishing. Thankfully, he was, and turned out to be a friendly bloke in his seventies who I'd spoken to once or twice before.

He agreed to come and see what I'd got and I couldn't hide my excitement on our way back down the path, explaining how I'd never caught a twenty-pounder but thought I'd finally got one. As we grew close, I moved into an eager trot and prepared for the moment of truth. After laying out my padded unhooking mat and filling a bucket with lake water, which I'd use to keep the fish protected, I heaved it out of the margin and over to the canvas with a grunt.

"Bloody 'ell," said my witness. "That might be a thirty." And I thought so too. This was an *immense* fish by my standards, and I cradled its bulky head in one hand while carefully removing the hook from its rubbery lower lip with my other. Now that smart phones had been invented, my next priority was to get photographic evidence of this mind-blowing capture. And with the light fading fast I was relieved that not only did my iPhone have a flash, but I had someone else to operate it.

Perhaps there was some vanity in my desperation to record that special moment in pixels, but most people who've spent many days and nights in purposeful, sometimes fruitless pursuit of large carp will understand. As did my friend, although he'd never come across a touchscreen before, which meant a hasty technical lesson while I also sloshed the carp with water and desperately tried to ensure it didn't slither off the mat and back towards the lake.

He eventually seemed to grasp the idea and I scrambled onto my knees behind the fish, initially struggling to get it off the ground but managing to place my hands correctly after a few attempts. I cradled it in awe and tried to savour the moment as my not-so-able assistant tried to get some shots.

I feared he wouldn't manage it, particularly when he mumbled something about 'modern technology' and asked if 'anything was happening', but to my immense relief he *did* capture several images of the mighty mirror – a framed copy of which can still be found in my parents' house.

With the modelling work done, I zipped the mat in order to weigh the carp and my companion held a torch. My arms shook as I raised the scales above my head and we watched the needle swing around the circular face – not once, but twice. That meant over thirty pounds and I could barely believe my eyes, although I was quickly reminded there was still the weight of the unhooking mat to detract.

I winced, knowing it must be accounting for at least a few of the pounds, but was still thrilled to have caught a new personal-best. It dwarfed my previous captures, no matter what the final weight might be, and we made a mental note of the figure before carrying the carp to the water's edge with the kind of reverence parents have for a new-born baby.

After letting the old gladiator slide back into the margin, it allowed me to hold it for a moment before swimming away slowly and steadily. Indeed, if you can believe a fish could swim with a 'swagger', this one did, as if letting me know I'd got lucky this time but it wouldn't happen again. I thanked it, the stars above and then the man who'd helped me, before returning to check the weight of the unhooking mat.

Once I'd subtracted it from the previous figure, I had to accept I'd not quite broken the thirty-pound barrier, but the fantastic fish had still weighed in at twenty-eight pounds, twelve ounces. It was my first twenty, and in some style, so I didn't dwell on the fact I'd been a bag of sugar away from cracking thirty. A quick, post-work session had produced something really special. Even if serious carp addicts now land forties and fifties on a fairly regular basis and the world record, caught recently in France, is a staggering one hundred and twelve pounds.

My late-spring capture was a tale I proudly recounted for several seasons to come, especially when arriving back at the lake and feeling every inch the 'local expert'. A stretch perhaps, but I became fairly proficient at specimen hunting during my early thirties and sometimes felt torn between my match fishing roots and this new, growing obsession that required different gear and entire weekends of endeavour.

For a short period, I managed to find enough time for both types of angling, accumulating a vast amount of tackle and experience in the process. I even spent one season on a private syndicate water, where there were several more forty-pounders to pursue, although I never did top my twenty-eight pound, twelve-ounce mirror carp. And before chasing big fish could take over completely, I became a father. At eight pounds, six ounces, Fred was the new catch of my life.

CHAPTER 16

Wilderness

Fred was a cherubic baby, always in the 'ninetieth percentile' of the growth charts, and during the hours of darkness he liked nothing more than screeching the house down. We received plenty of advice about colic, but the recommended cures, which ranged from cranial massage therapy to playing him the sound of vacuuming at night, never seemed to work.

Now I can see the first few months of insomnia for what they were – a fleeting moment in time – and the testing start has since been eclipsed by my son's good nature and affable charm, but it was a rude awakening to parenthood. My working life became relentless, too, not just for a few months but for the remainder of my thirties.

As a communications director who'd recently joined a start-up company with endless demands, and as a father to a beautiful son who slept like a dream all day only to spend the night wailing in his exhausted parents' arms, I entered a new and very different era of life – one with lots of joy but very little peace, sleep or, indeed, fishing.

The only angling-related benefit of working so hard came about with the company's international expansion, two or three years later. We opened an office in Toronto and, after getting to know the finance director during my first visit, she mentioned her husband was a keen fisherman and I should meet him next time I was over. Some months later, one dark October morning, I sat in the lobby of a Canadian hotel, bleary-eyed and still jet-lagged at the end of another busy week, waiting to do just that.

I was soon greeted by a friendly, talkative chap who promised me an introduction of a different kind – to the steelhead trout of the Beaver River. It was a fairly long drive to get there and we passed the time by swapping bankside stories, comparing notes and building up expectations for the day ahead. He explained we'd be using lures, or float fishing with mesh-bags filled with salmon roe, and he was good enough to lend me all the rods, tackle and waders required.

The ensuing trip was quite unlike anything else I've experienced. We first tackled up and slung rucksacks on our backs before making our way up the wild, boiling river, complete with snow-capped mountains in the distance. And we only saw one other human (a fellow fisherman) all day long. Thanks to my guide's expert help, I also managed to catch three majestic steelhead, a hard-fighting cousin of the brown trout, before we returned to the warmth of his car just as the sun went down.

Further company-related travels took me to Cape Town and European capitals such as Warsaw and Madrid, but I never managed any cheeky fishing trips like the one I enjoyed on the edge of the Canadian wilderness. Work was just too full-on, so I had to be content with maintaining a tenuous link with my old passion through reading books and grabbing the odd hour or two whenever I could.

I was still dedicated enough to continue my match visits to Sheffield every summer, but I was busy being a dad most other weekends. Even as Fred entered his third and fourth years, bringing his parents endless pride and amusement along the way, he was still too young for me to take fishing. But I did encourage him to have a dip with a bamboo-handled net during any family holidays.

He was inquisitive, fun-loving and full of character as a toddler, fascinated by his wooden train set, Postman Pat and a workbox of plastic tools. As an only child, he was also quite demanding and, whenever he wasn't recharging with a lengthy afternoon nap, he needed almost continual entertainment, exhausting Emma during the day and then moving his attention to me whenever he could.

Unfortunately, like so many working parents who commute into London, I often returned home too late to see him on weekdays, held up at the office or stuck on a slow train from Waterloo. But Fred's favourite weekend activities included den-building in the lounge, 'fixing' things with a plastic hammer or riding his bike, which he learned to do at a remarkably young age, on the local common.

Our terraced cottage, just off the village high street, was his playground, and he could often be found making his way up or down the steep stairs, thumb jammed in his mouth and Bob, his faithful and fraying teddy bear, dragging behind. The back garden was just about big enough to accommodate an inflatable paddling pool and, during the summer months, he loved splashing around in water.

On the rare occasions I managed to fish, I started to go with a good friend from work called Steve, who I'd first met in an office lift. We might never have got chatting if he hadn't overheard the end of a call about a big carp I'd caught recently, but he did, and by the time we reached the upper floors where Steve worked in the finance department, we were comparing pictures on our phones.

I'd discovered a fellow, if also semi-retired carp addict and we kept in touch after eventually moving on from the company. A few years later, by then fathers and living only a few miles apart, it seemed natural for us to join forces in a bid to keep the fishing flame alight. And we did manage a handful of trips – including a couple of memorable visits to a lovely estate lake at Bury Hill, near Dorking.

It's a glorious and relatively well-known fishery, having featured in a few TV programmes and being graced by several of angling's biggest personalities, so it made a rather special and decadent escape for two weary workers. Catching fish became secondary to simply swapping stressed-out offices and commuter trains for country air and stunning surroundings.

We also enjoyed a bottle of beer and usually talked nonsense for the few precious hours we had. It's often said there's a child within most men, and I think the ratio must be high for those who fish, because, while we were too old for icy swimming dares, I remember our outings for their silliness rather than any fish we caught.

During one such session at Bury Hill, we ended the day without a bite between us but didn't care after cracking up over an unexpected joke – our hastily prepared packed lunches. We'd seized the opportunity of a Sunday outing with little notice – grabbing our tackle, bait and whatever food was in our respective fridges with little thought – so only once our patience with the fish began to fray did we reach into our bags to remind ourselves what was on offer.

It turned out we had no sandwiches, crisps or chocolate bars between us – staples of most angling packed lunches – but instead fell about laughing after producing a collection of middle-class goodies more suited to the Henley Regatta. Our pooled resources included a tub of marinated olives and feta, some artichokes, assorted cured meats, a selection of fine cheeses and half a bottle of wine – a culinary spread to surpass all others on the lake that day and an amusing, if slightly cringeworthy reminder of how long we'd both been living in Surrey.

CHAPTER 17

Breaking Strain

Settling down in the south led to some fantastic experiences, new friends and career opportunities, but the pressure of working in London came with challenges too. Commuting to the capital every day, in addition to the breakneck pace of growth at my firm, meant I often got home exhausted and still fending off calls.

I often didn't get to read Fred a bedtime story and, on those nights, could only creep into his bedroom, give him a heartfelt peck on the cheek and listen to his gentle breathing for a while. Even weekends rarely passed without interruption and I was regularly, perhaps rightfully, chided for continually looking at my phone.

Emma had her hands full with Fred, especially with no relatives living nearby, and our time was increasingly spent apart. Sadly, just a few years after our son came into our world, it sometimes felt like we were living separate lives. There were still many highs and lots of wonderful memories, but I sometimes stopped to wonder what had become of two school friends who'd fallen in love and got married eight years previously.

Our lovely boy provided shared happiness and a family bond between us all that will never end, but as he turned four it was hard to deny his parents had grown apart. And I suppose relationship clichés like that exist for a reason – how else can I explain something that happened which would've seemed impossible just a year or two before?

Although I could never have contemplated or anticipated the end of our marriage during the majority of our time together, we ended up separating and, after two years of focusing on Fred's adjustment to the new situation, we eventually divorced. We were still his mum and dad and managed to keep things amicable, but I suddenly found myself back in a one-bedroom flat in Woking town centre, trying to cope with overwhelming grief and adapting to life as a weekend-dad.

The first year alone was undoubtedly the hardest, bleakest of my life – including a Christmas Day spent drinking too much in an almost-deserted block of flats – but most weekends brought a burst of sunshine into my gloom, as Fred arrived to spend a couple of nights with me. Initially, he slept in a temporary bed, usually after we'd enjoyed some Chinese food and one of his favourite films, although he later adopted my sofa as his preferred place of rest.

He usually fell asleep by my side, after which I'd watch another hour of TV, or work on a laptop before seeking my own bed. I needed every bit of sleep I could get, because he always rose at the crack of dawn – full of beans and ready for action. Sometimes he'd insist on watching *Casper the Friendly Ghost* for an hour or two, or want to play on his Nintendo, but most of our time was spent outdoors. We staged regular sword fights, kicked footballs, attempted to fly kites and explored the local cut by bike.

His mum has amazing strength and is one of the most brilliant, caring people I know, so we worked hard to remain close and still shared things like Fred's birthdays and sports days. Our precious weekends together brought much-needed pleasure into my world, too, although I still wrestled with the guilt and sadness of a failed marriage. I also continued to work long hours, especially with two sets of bills to pay, but we shared so much fun before each Sunday evening brought a painful farewell.

Being in a small apartment again, my fishing gear was kept in a plastic storage shed on the mossy balcony beside the lounge. And there it remained, largely untouched, until Fred turned five. Only during our second summer there did I wake one morning with the exciting idea that he might be ready to try fishing, so after breakfast we drove to Goldsworth Angling.

There I bought a cheap, telescopic pole, half a pint of maggots and a float that Fred chose himself. And while our impulsive shopping trip wasn't quite so memorable as when I received Granddad's cigar box, my lad seemed up for it and I felt a prickle of excitement as we arrived back at the flat to prepare. I hurriedly made packed lunches and found our picnic blanket before I headed outside again, holding Fred's chubby hand as we made our way to the canal.

It was red hot and the park was busy with dogs,

children playing cricket and identikit teenagers hanging around the skate ramps, so we went a fair way along the path to find a bit of peace. I eventually found somewhere a little less chaotic and lay the blanket on the ground near a patch of lilies. They looked like they might hold a few fish and should be within Fred's reach.

After tackling up slowly, feeling quite rusty after so long away from fishing, I handed Fred the pole and showed him how to swing out the simple rig, which he mastered after a few minutes of trial and error. Once the float was in position, he obediently watched it as I tried to explain, probably far too quickly, that we were now waiting for a bite and, if the tip should disappear, he would need to strike.

He looked up at me, nodding and smiling, which is when the magnitude of our seemingly insignificant endeavour hit me. Anyone passing by wouldn't have given us a second look, but here I was – thirty or so years since I'd first settled down on a canvas stool at The Pond – crouching next to my son and telling him to watch out for bites, just as Granddad had instructed me. That emotional moment of realisation, probably encompassing everything else significant that had happened over three decades, was almost too much for me and I fought back tears so as not to alarm Fred.

I had no idea if he was feeling any of the 'wonder' I'd experienced on a similar June day so very long ago, or whether he'd go on to be an angler, but it didn't really matter. I was content just watching him, as he clutched his new pole and squinted against the glare while we hoped for a fish to bite. We'd gone to sleep on what felt like any other Friday night, yet here we were, twelve or so hours later, on Fred's inaugural trip – and it's no exaggeration to say that life felt good again.

He maintained concentration for five minutes,

which was quite something at that age, before asking if he should move the float. I suggested he should give it a bit longer, before scattering a few more maggots near the pads. I also took a quick snap on my phone, so that I could proudly share the moment with a few family members and friends, and by the time I'd done that he was getting a little twitchy.

Luckily, his impatience soon evaporated, as the orange float registered a succession of tentative nibbles. I responded excitedly, telling him to get ready for the float to go under, and a few seconds later it was towed sideways and then beneath.

Fred lifted his pole sharply and was amazed to see a tiddler come flying out of the water, just I had been at Moorwood Lane. I cheered and laughed, while my little lad beamed and jerked his head backwards, trying to avoid the alien creature now swinging around his face. It was the mirror image of my first capture, although Fred's fish was barely an ounce in weight and, rather than the silver flash of a roach, it bore the green scales and delicate black stripes of a juvenile perch.

No matter the size or species, Fred had done it. He'd caught his first fish, and on the first cast of his first trip, almost without assistance. Just as I had, he studied the tiny creature as it lay in my outstretched palm. At least until it jumped, which made him jump too. Shocked by the sudden movement, he begged me to get rid of it, but I persuaded him we should take a picture first – somehow holding my phone with one hand and the fish in my other, while also getting Fred in the frame, smiling proudly in the background.

After slipping the perch back I gave him a high-five and he went on to land a few more of them, plus some roach and even a rudd during that memorable excursion. None of them weighed more than two ounces, but I saw delight in my son's eyes as his confidence grew. It was enough to hold his attention for at least another hour, which was quite something for Fred. Especially once he plucked up the courage to hold a few of the fish for himself – feeling a fleeting but direct connection with something wild and alive, before watching them swim away.

CHAPTER 18

African Adventure

Catching fish can be relatively simple or extremely tricky, and can therefore mean many different things to the millions of people who regard it as an integral part of their lives. I am no exception, and being in angling's magic circle has brought me immeasurable happiness, excitement, peace and a deep appreciation of nature. It has also helped create strong family bonds and several friendships to last a lifetime.

Every time I go fishing – whether snatching a couple of hours or taking part in a match, and no matter if I'm successful or not – I'm semi-conscious that I'm creating another mosaic of subtle memories that will join countless others already locked away. And as for those rare trips when the stars seem to align and everything goes perfectly, I'll still be replaying those if I ever get too frail to go. That's how strongly a handful of 'red letter' days have been tattooed in my mind.

For many people around the world who rely on fishing as a way of life, it's a serious business – a dangerous but essential source of food or income. And even for those lucky enough to be pleasure anglers, it can become an obsession. Whether one's dream is to catch the biggest specimen, find the perfect venue or compete at the highest level, it's something that can occupy the mind, body and soul. Some merely seek solitude, relaxation or fresh air, and thankfully there is no right or wrong way to enjoy it.

Few in the UK manage to become professional anglers, although they do exist, and there's no doubt that having the necessary instincts, ability and dedication to make it one's job is an admirable achievement. Yet many who fish infrequently cherish their hobby, particularly the social side, just as dearly. Whether meeting with like-minded individuals at events, as part of a club, or simply by chance at the waterside, it's a common bond that transcends social class, gender, ethnicity, experience, age and any other theoretical divide one may care to suggest.

I've met many anglers over the years with whom I'm sure I could have become good friends, easily striking up conversation and enjoying a good laugh, only to part with a mutual farewell of "tight lines" and no idea if our paths will ever cross again. Occasionally they do, and I'd much rather spend my days recognising long-lost but familiar faces while wandering riverbanks than gradually spotting regulars in a steamy commuter carriage. If I could choose.

I cherish all these aspects of fishing and more, but during a difficult period in my thirties I can honestly say that my passion did something extraordinary for me. It still feels strange to claim, but fishing *saved* me. Saved me from what is harder to define, but let's just say I was close to the edge.

Close to burnout, as they say in the business world – because I was still adapting to life as a single dad and wrestling with my new reality as the work pressure continued to pile on. And it eventually got to the point where it, whatever it may be, felt all-consuming.

One of my younger brothers is a fireman, while his wife is a nurse, so I'm well aware that the stress of an office job should not be overstated or invoke too much sympathy – not when others face injury or care for those in pain on a regular basis – but for a whole host of reasons I'd reached a point where, I believe, I was close to experiencing what some might call a breakdown.

Burnout is now recognised as a medical phenomenon of the 21st century and, looking back, I was certainly showing many of the symptoms. I was emotionally fragile, mentally agitated and struggling to sleep. I became anxious about many things, unable to focus for very long, and felt increasingly worn out from insomnia and persistent stress.

I was so exhausted I once went completely blank, somehow asleep and awake at the same time, in an important meeting at work. Thankfully, a mentor who knew something of what I was going through was quick to recognise I was seriously unwell and sent me home to rest. I stumbled through the tube and train home in a daze, while receiving several texts and voicemails urging me to see a doctor.

I took the advice and received some strong sleeping tablets that finally knocked me out for a night. Sleep was all I wanted for several days, but my concerned colleagues and family stayed in touch and urged me to go on long hikes in the wintry countryside. I walked for miles, my breath clouding around my head like the muddled thoughts inside it, and strode on until I was physically knackered too. Yet nothing seemed to ease the pressure I felt, real or perceived, in a more permanent way.

I appreciated the week off but, before returning to work, I realised that I probably needed a proper break. Not a holiday with friends, or even with Fred, but a way of completely removing myself from work, pressure, society, electronics and everything that had come to dominate my waking hours. I'd never had such a holiday and didn't really know if they existed, but after easing my way back into the weekday routine I was lucky enough to start chatting to a colleague who knew about my love of fishing.

He suggested I should go on an angling adventure or 'safari' as he put it. Not to retreat to some caravan park in Devon, or a secluded cottage in the New Forest, but to fly somewhere new, exotic and miles from anything resembling London. After a quick Google I discovered a specialist travel company offering group trips to The Gambia in West Africa. The website was pretty basic but promised sunshine, deep blue sea, spectacular 'big game' fish and, most importantly, no mobile masts in sight.

I hadn't turned off my work phone in six or seven years, and I hadn't been fishing for months either, so I made a tentative call to establish whether I could afford such a trip. After chatting to the company's owner for half an hour I dared hope for salvation, and he told me to expect a DVD about the experiences they organised. He also reassured me I could join an existing party of two or three anglers to help keep the cost down.

I naturally tried Andy and Steve, gently pitching the idea of gigantic fish and ten days away from it all, but I was hardly shocked when they confirmed it would be impossible to get time off to join me. I completely understood, of course, particularly as I'd not managed a holiday of more than a week for several years myself, most of which had been interrupted by work issues anyway, but I'd unfortunately reached a point where I couldn't afford *not* to take time off. Or to do whatever else it took to regain some calm and perspective.

Several months later – and only after swallowing a crushing, last-minute work request to cancel my first booking due to another business crisis – I finally boarded a plane. It was destined for Casablanca, where we stopped briefly, before changing flights and leaving for The Gambia. Once there, I met the handful of fellow anglers joining me for the adventure and we chatted briefly before piling into a beaten-up Land Rover and bouncing along seemingly endless dirt roads.

We passed through a scorched, amber landscape that was all new to me and helped drive home the fact I'd finally made it to West Africa. Upon reaching our destination, slightly bruised, thirsty and disorientated, I sat alone and unpacked my suitcase in a basic, whitewashed hotel room.

Despite splitting the cost with two strangers, I was lucky enough not to be sharing, so I relished the quiet, relatively cool sanctuary following the long and fairly complex journey to get there. For the first time in months I felt a moment of tranquillity, although I do remember instinctively reaching for my phone and feeling a familiar jolt of apprehension as I went to check it for messages.

To my great relief, and despite plentiful pre-travel warnings, I was surprised to see no reception bars. Even though I was there to recharge, the well-trained urge to know what was going on, and whether I was being asked for anything important, was still there.

Only removing the option completely allowed me to relax – for now at least, because I'd been told there was some unreliable Wi-Fi in the reception area. Even that didn't matter for now, I told myself, because most of the trip would be spent aboard a boat and maybe, just *maybe*, I'd follow the doctor's orders and turn everything off for ten days.

Despite my new surroundings and many hours spent in the air, I slept deeply that first night, laying undisturbed under a creaking ceiling fan and only waking when an early alarm signalled a start to the fishing. I first met my new friends again at breakfast and learned one of them, a retired professor who'd taught at Sheffield University, had been on a couple of these trips before. They were his annual break from his otherwise-continual and admirable role as a carer, and husband, for his severely disabled wife.

We soon hit it off, despite a huge age gap, and were still chatting excitedly when our guides Pepe and Max arrived. They introduced themselves and completed a group of six men who would soon be spending a *lot* of time together. Pepe (pronounced Peepee) was Gambian and therefore spoke good English, yet he seemed strangely familiar in some other way.

I'm very good at walking straight past A-list celebrities in London – only for a friend to stare back in amazement and say, "Oh my god, did you see such-and-such?" while I shake my head and say, "Really?" So it took a few minutes to click. Eventually, I realised I'd seen his intelligent eyes and friendly smile on TV – in Robson Green's *Extreme Fishing* series, which I explained giddily, like a star-struck teenager, to my new friends.

Pepe had clearly guided more than one *Extreme Fishing* fan and took my babbling questions with good grace, but he seemed interested to learn that I lived in Surrey and had once passed Robson Green, who lived in the next village along at the time, while on a bike ride with Fred.

Mr Green had been cycling with a young passenger, too, but, along with our northern accents, it didn't seem enough common ground to request a selfie or exchange numbers at the time. Putting that to one side, I learned that Pepe had given Robson some cash for a laptop, which had apparently never materialised, likely due to some genuine mix-up, so I promised to nudge the Geordie actor and singer if I should ever see him again!

Max was from Senegal and spoke only a little English, which he did with a thick French accent and an infectious grin. We shook hands and then drove along the coast for an hour, through bustling villages and more scrubland, before arriving at a picturesque bay that was home to many colourful, wooden fishing boats. Our two vessels were the only ones made of fibreglass, both of them equipped with powerful-looking, twin Honda outboards.

Otherwise, they seemed like a fairly rudimentary craft, with an open cabin towards the front and a canvas awning over the decks. Pepe explained that the Prof and I would use one boat, along with him and Max, whereas the other two anglers would meet their guides on the other.

The water was shallow enough for us all to wade to and fro in our flip flops, or bare feet, carrying heavy freezer boxes from the beach to the boats. They were full of drinking water and a few beers, accompanied by battered cans of diesel fuel, crates of food and armfuls of fishing rods.

After several trips, watched by half-interested professional fishermen tending their traditional boats, we finally clambered aboard and surveyed what would be our new home until nightfall. I noticed a series of sloping, metal tubes in either side of the gunwale that would soon hold the butts of the formidable rods we'd be using, which I'd been told were capable of handling anything from crevalle jack to a variety of sharks.

Once we'd said goodbye to our companions and pulled up the anchors, Max pushed us further out across the shallow flats, before hauling himself over the side and starting the engines. He was soaked up to his chest, but his vest and shorts would dry out in minutes once re-exposed to the fierce African sun and a fresh breeze of our own making.

After his assistant had started the engine, Pepe slowly steered us clear of the remaining boats, before pushing the throttle forward and propelling us further away with surprising force. The bow lifted up and started to smack against countless small waves – bouncing us towards the horizon while we held onto the rails at the rear, continually sprayed by saltwater and laughing like kids.

As we reached the open sea and slowed down to a more steady pace I slapped on more sun cream, adjusted my sunglasses, pulled on a baseball cap, checked my lifejacket fastening and tried not to weep with joy. But there was no doubting this was a moving experience. We were on our way to the continental shelf, in search of ocean-going monsters, and I felt no stress, just sheer exhilaration as we moved further away from land.

I didn't think things could get much better, but soon Max was pointing starboard and shouting in French. I turned my head and saw we'd been joined by a small pod of dolphins. They chased us for twenty minutes, jumping and rolling repeatedly only a few feet from the hull, and I soon decided they looked as happy and free as I suddenly felt. We all yelled in delight and even shook hands at times, never growing tired of watching such amazing creatures in the unbeatable high definition of real life.

Later that morning, and indeed during every magical morning of the trip, we tackled up our rods with industrial strength line and hooks, before sending big chunks of fish down into the depths, or trawling giant lures behind the boat. We were in search of awe-inspiring, hard-fighting and beautiful species such as mahi-mahi, wahoo or, in one unforgettable encounter, sailfish.

Growing up to ten feet long and reckoned to be the world's fastest fish, the sailfish is a member of the marlin family. And not only do they have an impressive spear with which to hunt, they get their name from a huge dorsal fin that enables them to make dramatic manoeuvres while chasing fast-moving prey, or indeed while escaping from devastated anglers.

They're famous for spectacular battles, often featuring several searing runs and breath-taking, acrobatic leaps, so are naturally one of the most sought-after pelagic species. Growing up in Sheffield or living in Surrey, I'd never once imagined trying to catch one, or at least not with any serious hope, but I got my unexpected chance when the Prof connected with something massive during a dramatic last day at sea.

Like mine, his rod tip had been thrumming for hours, gently curved over by the resistance of a lure being worked far behind the boat, but it hadn't once signalled any predatory interest. In fact, we'd had four rods out since mid-morning, all trawling imitation prey a few feet below the shimmering surface, and none of us had seen any follows, strikes or other signs of action all day.

It was looking like our first blank of the holiday – a bit hard to stomach seeing as we had to leave the following morning – and we were feeling as close to boredom as it's possible to get off the coast of West Africa. Our skipper's expertise and everyone's persistence eventually paid off, however, when the Prof's rod wrenched over without warning and the screaming reel was shrill enough to cut through the chugging engines.

Both he and Max scrambled to get hold of the bucking rod and, just as he managed to do so, we saw a glinting spear – dark against the distant waves and shaking wildly in an attempt to shed the hook. "Sailfish!" yelled Pepe.

"Oh my god" was the only response his bewildered, older customer could muster, while I swore repeatedly in disbelief. My friend could barely get the rod above horizontal, such was the strength of the take, and Max was soon having to help, meaning there were two pairs of hands now trying to cushion the braided line as it left the spool at an insane and seemingly unstoppable rate. I could see where it entered the water, many yards away, and watched it zipping through the surface, leaving a fizzing wake like a miniature speedboat, as the big fish veered away.

Pepe scrambled to fetch a fighting harness from the cabin and Max took the strain for a moment, so the Prof could get into it. Our guide was younger and stronger than the rest of us, but still gritted his teeth and placed his feet wide apart before leaning back with every muscle straining.

Pepe helped my awestruck companion get his arms through the straps before clipping each side of the harness into holes on either side of the rasping reel. The butt of the rod was then wrestled into a plastic cup against the Prof's belly, so he was able to use his shoulders and back a little more effectively.

The sailfish was soon living up to its impressive reputation – repeatedly leaping, cartwheeling and twisting through the air, and now at an alarming distance from the boat. At times it appeared more like an illusion, and every breach drew subconscious gasps from the near-helpless onlookers.

Max tried to help his customer regain some control, because he was now sweating profusely, asking for water and looking a little flushed. I offered verbal encouragement while both men held on for dear life, swearing and shaking their heads as yet another violent dash began.

It took another fifteen draining minutes for the duo to regain any line and it was only the assistance of Max that made it possible. By this stage the Prof had to sit down and was panting with exertion, before looking at me and begging for a break. I could tell he was serious and I agreed to take over, so we went through another tricky, almost comedic process of transferring the harness and heaving rod to another person.

As we did so, I felt excited and worried in equal measure – adrenaline combined with cold fear that I might lose this incredible fish that had almost broken the original angler. Once in the hot seat, I confirmed I was ready, tensing my body in anticipation. Max let go of the rod and I felt the incredible power of the sailfish for the first time.

It was now deep down, somewhere fairly near the boat, and I was advised to 'pump and wind', repeatedly heaving the rod tip upwards before winding furiously to regain line as it came back down. That way I was able to keep some measure of control and not allow things to go dangerously slack, but it was more draining than any gym workout.

So much braid had been taken in the early stages that I was soon drenched in sweat and trying to ignore a growing ache in my arms and back that threatened to leave me slumped uselessly next to the professor. The fight went on and on, and I gained a new appreciation for the pain of Santiago's epic encounter with a giant marlin in Hemingway's *The Old Man and the Sea*.

Not until well past the half-hour mark, and only after making a final dash for the horizon, did the magnificent fish noticeably start to tire. It eventually came close the surface and stayed there, which is when I was able to cautiously draw the slanting line nearer to Max's outstretched and gloved hand.

He strained to grab hold of the taut leader, with the sailfish just ten or twelve feet below the surface, and leaned so far over the side I felt sure he would topple in, right next to the deadly looking bill. Once the thick nylon and steel swivel came within touching distance, he made one more stretch and managed to grasp it, expertly twisting his hand to ensure a couple of turns were looped around it.

By this time, Pepe was holding onto his waistband and both of them heaved to try and bring the sailfish right up to the surface. Their combined strength was enough and at last we could claim an authentic catch – leading to shouts of triumph and a rush of jubilation that was shared equally amongst all of us.

I don't expect I'll ever witness a more breath-taking capture. As the giant fish rolled onto its side, its huge dorsal fin splayed out in all its glory and electric waves of colour flashed and rippled along its flanks. Iridescent blue and purple light pulsed in fleeting stripes while a big, baleful eye looked up at us through the crystal water. I looked back in dumbfounded wonder and could only pat the Prof on the back, both our legs shaking with exertion and clothes sodden with sweat.

The next few minutes were turbulent, but Max and Pepe got hold of the spear at one end and a scimitar-like tail at the other, somehow lifting the fish aboard briefly to be unhooked and then held reverently by its combined captors. We were unable to weigh it, but no one cared, and our next priority was to tag and safely return the mighty fish to the water.

Once lowered overboard, Max again held the bill in his gloved hand and Pepe gently eased the boat forward, pulling the fish alongside and forcing water back through its gills. We rested our exhausted arms on the side and watched its long body begin to recover, moving more forcefully and sweeping its tail steadily, before Max decided it was ready and let go.

He used the final moment of contact to push the huge, shimmering head away from the boat, before slapping the surface in celebration. The fish dropped away as we continued to move forward, but treated us to a final, defiant flash of light along its sides before diving back to freedom.

We couldn't stop smiling for an hour afterwards, meaning our facial muscles were soon as tired as the rest of our bodies. We were overflowing with delight and Pepe opened some celebratory beers for the homeward journey. As we savoured the cold drinks, clinking bottles and gaining speed once more, it was surely the high-point of an already unforgettable trip.

My emergency break not only introduced me to a new country, friends and incredible species of fish, it also saved me from something quite dark and dangerous. I followed the doctor's orders and, by the time I got home, felt revitalised.

I had lots of photos on my iPhone and countless memories but, more importantly, I also had a new appreciation for the importance of mental health, rest and recuperation. Adult life is rarely plain sailing and there were still some major challenges to come, but going to The Gambia for ten days had meant I was stronger, wiser and – most important of all – more grateful than ever for the magic of fishing.

CHAPTER 19

Commercialism

Despite winning my first DWSSC trophy thanks to a generous slice of luck, it was almost like a curse was lifted and I went on to do well in many more matches during my late teens – and indeed throughout my twenties and thirties.

As I entered my forties, some aspects of competitive fishing, and indeed life, had changed beyond recognition, but I still made several 360-mile round trips every summer. I was always eager to re-join Andy, Peter and all of our matchday friends, even if our numbers were shrinking and we no longer visited my beloved Trent.

We stopped using coaches to pick us up from the clubhouse as well, for financial reasons, but continued to meet for breakfast somewhere near the venue, before handing over our pools money and eagerly awaiting the draw. I still found it hard to sleep the night before, too, despite the fact I was usually dog-tired from a hectic working week and the sluggish drive up from Woking.

Grandma was approaching ninety and living with dementia, which slowly robbed her of short-term memory, but once I'd parked on Downing Road and knocked at the porch we still had the same talcum-scented hugs. They just became a little weaker each time, and in her final two years in the house she struggled to look after me as she'd always done.

I started to eat in motorway service stations on the way there and also brought my own packed lunches, telling her not to fuss and repeatedly offering reassurances that I wasn't hungry. Still, she insisted on fetching the drinks and tried to work the remote control so we could watch the weather forecast.

We increasingly had the same conversations on a constant loop, but I didn't mind answering her simple questions up to ten or twelve times. I found new ways to describe my work and update her about Fred, or I'd add different details each time to keep myself genuinely engaged.

Sometimes her fading mental connections flickered back to life, and she briefly realised what was happening. She would apologise and chide herself, but I'd simply switch the subject to more distant times, when her older, deeper memories would flood back and the conversations became more animated and happy again.

By this stage, the single bed in the spare room really was struggling to hold my man-sized frame, regularly lurching over and sometimes tipping me out, but I didn't mind that either. So much was different since my childhood stays, except for that bed and that room.

Even Humbug, an ancient, knitted bear, still sat on the bedside table, along with a wind-up travel clock from the 1970s and a cotton doily for my glass of water.

It was still a welcome, comforting sanctuary and no matter what was happening in the rest of the world, once I'd wished Grandma goodnight and made sure she'd got to her room, I could get undressed, set my alarm and begin to look forward to the following day.

She no longer got up to wish me goodbye in the mornings, perhaps forgetting that I was staying there, but I liked to leave her a little note in the kitchen, thanking her for the hospitality and promising to let her know how I got on. Then I'd steal out through the porch, pushing the key back through the letterbox before making the short but familiar walk down the passage to my car.

I missed driving to meet everyone at the clubhouse in Dronfield Woodhouse and there were actually times when it would have been much easier to get to a match rendezvous from Mum and Dad's, but it felt good to have spent the night with Grandma. And leaving her house early on summer mornings still added to the many threads of nostalgia woven through each trip.

The matches were, and still are, held on a growing number of commercial fisheries around South Yorkshire, Lincolnshire and Nottinghamshire – including some unusually named places like Candy Corner, Swanlands and Messingham Sands. They were always heavily stocked and featured accessible banks that allowed the older members to park behind their pegs and fish from stable platforms. Bites were plentiful, often from hard-fighting carp, and so our tactics and baits evolved too.

Gone were the days of bringing buckets of maggots or hemp and fishing with stick floats, wagglers or traditional swimfeeders. Instead, in came strong carbon poles, 'method feeders' and two or three keepnets in case we had a particularly good day. Baits ranged from sweetcorn and luncheon meat, to hard pellets and fishmeal groundbait – most of them coming out of supermarket tins or plastic packaging bearing a growing number of slick new brand names.

No longer would a few pounds of fish put me in the frame, either. Our informal matches were regularly being won with sixty, seventy or even a hundred pounds of carp by then. And they were still *small* weights compared to the open or semi-professional match circuits, where hundreds of pounds were often needed. Still, we were a million metaphorical miles from the early matches, where seven or eight pounds of hard-won skimmers, chub or roach was often enough to claim victory on the Trent.

Commercials also required a different kind of knowledge, skill and watercraft, which I seemed fairly proficient at. While I missed the mystery and rugged scenery of the Trent – especially the early morning arrivals, when steam rose invitingly from the warm and powerful flow – I couldn't knock the non-stop action we enjoyed if the ponds we now fished were in good form.

I eventually broke the old-fashioned 'ton' (100lb) barrier and performed consistently enough that my name is engraved several times in succession on the base of DWSSC's overall winner's trophy. It's a grand silver one that's been presented to the angler with the biggest combined weight of fish, across each season's matches, for over half a century.

Not that it was all about winning. The people and the fishing were always far more important aspects of any matchday and during all the years fishing with DWSSC I continually wished the many people could, somehow, continue their attendance with me. It was they who kept me in touch with treasured memories and feelings from my youth, and therefore always saddening when I was informed that another well-known character would now be absent.

It's never felt fair that people, and everything they represent or mean to me, can't carry on forever – but I'm not Peter Pan and of course they can't. Grandma maintained her independence almost right until the end, only moving to a care home for the final year or so of her life. I drove up and visited her there a couple of days before she died, and she still recognised me, along with my brother, Sam.

We were both on the verge of tears by the time we left, knowing how terribly weak and tired she was, but we consoled ourselves that at least she was sleeping all the time and seemed to be comfortable. After saying an awkward goodbye, I cried all the way back to Surrey, banging the steering wheel, swearing out loud and knowing I wouldn't see that amazing woman again.

It can feel impossibly hard to come to terms with the death of a loved one and everything associated with them. Losing Granddad had been a terrible blow that took years to accept, but now Grandma had gone and that meant losing Downing Road as well.

Despite the fact my mum and dad held onto the house for a number of years, it was rented out to strangers and never again would I park outside, knock on the porch or spend a night dreaming about the perfect fishing trip in my wonky bed. At times, it felt like the heavy grief would be a permanent presence, because another vital link to a simpler, more innocent period was broken, yet as one epic chapter came to a close, a new one naturally began.

I continued to travel up for the matches and began staying at my parents' house instead – usually in Sam's old room, rather than my own. I generally arrived in Sheffield late on a Thursday night and if I made it by 10.30pm there was usually time to have a quick drink – with Dad, Sam, Joe and my brother-in-law, Bob – before driving the final extra minutes to see Mum.

They often met in the same pub, following an evening game of five-a-side football and, sure enough, over time, that little ritual became increasingly familiar – a new sign that another matchday weekend had begun. Sitting down in The Rising Sun, sipping a pint and catching up on news, I always knew the tedious traffic jams had been worth it. I wasn't hallucinating and I really had made it back for another precious day out with the club.

They still held much of their original appeal but I was also back in Sheffield to catch up with my family, including a growing tribe of nieces and nephews, and to stay with my amazing folks. That usually meant working from their spare room all Friday, before snapping my laptop shut around 6pm and heading down to the garage to prepare for the following morning.

While most of the original members had long since departed to the great river in the sky, Andy and his dad were my constant DWSSC companions as we explored numerous fisheries and honed our commercial skills with every passing year. Even Peter, despite his advancing age, managed to win a couple of matches, and I'm sure if they were drivers in the same Formula 1 team Andy would have happily let him 'pass by' in every race.

The three of us always met for breakfast – everywhere from a Morrison's supermarket café just off Sheffield Parkway, to a wide range of on-site fishery facilities – which allowed us to jointly relish the prospect of another match and share thoughts on how we'd approach it. We also relived successes, failures and amusing anecdotes from the past, which now stretched out far behind us.

They included numerous legendary, to us at least, tales – such as the time the roof of a double-decker bus we were travelling on hit the underside of a bridge.

That could have been deadly, we knew, but thankfully it was just the biggest shock that twenty sleepy anglers had ever received.

Or the few occasions when fellow members had watched their rod pulled in by a powerful fish, or even gone in for an unintended swim themselves. We never grew tired of such retellings and each of us understood they, and we, were part of a tiny, seemingly-insignificant but wonderful thread of history.

It was therefore heart-breaking when I learned that Peter had passed, just a few years ago, and I realised another friend and a much-loved figure from my adolescence would no longer be there to greet me warmly at the start of the following season. He had enjoyed life and managed a decent innings, but knowing he was gone affected me far more than I might have expected.

He'd been such a constant and reassuring presence throughout my fishing odyssey, just like Granddad had been to begin with. Not just driving Andy and I to numerous junior matches or dropping us off at Oakley's to buy yet more tackle, but eventually becoming part of the human fabric of a club that had been a steady and blissful part of my existence for so long.

For Andy it was the loss of his dad, and naturally much harder to bear, but I shared some of his pain from miles away and tried to offer words of encouragement whenever I could – often via WhatsApp messages from the banks of a Surrey lake or river, when I sent pictures of any captures and let him know which tactics were working, before asking how he was coping.

He's a brave lad, but on the morning of the first match of the following season we both fell quiet upon meeting, briefly struggling for words. It was the first one for many years that Andy had driven himself to, rather than joining his dad for a lift, and even the sight of an unfamiliar car had rocked me.

He wasn't alone, however, because Harry, his young son and Peter's grandson, was mercifully with him too. Aged only six or seven at the time, he was entering his second season of the club matches, helped to enjoy them by his patient father, and was becoming an increasingly keen, albeit small and rather shy angler.

Soon after shaking hands, we entered a farm shop and were quickly engulfed by the chatter of other matchmen, along with the smell of frying bacon and fresh coffee. Harry sat quietly with Andy and me, letting us tease him about the modest size of his breakfast. I made a joke about using any leftover sausages for bait and he smiled in response, which is when it struck me: history was repeating itself again.

Peter was no longer with us and, somehow, I was now the slightly unfamiliar and relatively old man offering encouragement and pulling the leg of a young'un over a pre-match breakfast. For one dizzying moment, I felt tempted to offer a slice of white bread from the basket placed on the table between us, but decided that was one little tradition that needn't live on.

Instead, I gently challenged him to try and beat me, asking what tactics he had in mind and which peg he might want to draw. We weren't sitting on a swaying coach, but once again I marvelled at the poignancy of what was taking place – feeling the distant echoes bounce back through the years to be amplified by my mouth. And for the second time, I suddenly understood that with the unbearably sad closure of one chapter, another happy one was about to begin.

CHAPTER 20

Lost and Found

Having lived in my rented apartment for a couple of years, slowly adapting to the seismic change while gaining ever-more enjoyment and pride from my time with Fred, I experienced another rebirth of sorts. For once it wasn't related to my son or fishing, however; this time I fell in love.

Rachel and I had first met well over a decade earlier, as she became my new manager when I moved to Woking. With a shared enjoyment of PR and the odd social evening with our teammates, she helped me settle into the new job, office and town.

We always got on well as colleagues and friends, but we only worked together for a few more years before parting ways for a similar, if not longer period. Our paths didn't cross again for a long time and under different, more difficult circumstances. By then, each of us had long-term relationships that had either ended or were breaking down, plus we both had young children.

A chance meeting at a work-related reunion, therefore, seemed nothing more than an opportunity to catch up, reminisce and offer some mutual words of support for the stress we were both experiencing. But although our individual circumstances were different in ways, we recognised enough common ground – and shared memories – to stay in touch.

Not very often to begin with, but our previous friendship, combined with the emotional help we were now able to provide each other with, meant our relationship eventually turned into something far more complicated and powerful. Meeting for an occasional coffee or evening drink, we found the company, empathy and occasional laughter remarkably comforting.

After a while, even half an hour spent chatting over the phone made me feel deliriously happy and during the course of several months we formed much deeper feelings for each other. I fell for her hard and, despite the seemingly impossible challenges and undoubted heartache of the changes occurring in our lives, our growing romance eclipsed the previous friendship.

She is a beautiful, incredible person, so my need to spend more time together grew by the month. And once we'd acknowledged the situation more openly, and were living in separate rented properties less than a mile apart, we dated more regularly for a year. We were painfully aware that our children had already been through a lot of upheaval, however, and still didn't know if or how we'd resolve our desire to be united.

They say love conquers all, but it was also financial prudence that eventually broke the deadlock. Or at least it helped us make up our minds, because we decided to pool our remaining resources, stop wasting money on rent and buy a house together. It was a huge leap of faith, having never spent more than a night or two under the same roof, and with another big change for our combined children to consider, but our feelings remained unshakeable and so we set about sizing up the local property market.

Initially, this was a depressing experience, due to the fact we were looking for something with the potential to accommodate two adults and four children, while also needing to remain close to our ex-partners. Surrey is not the cheapest place to live and I once again found my northern sensibilities offended as our bids on a string of houses spiralled well beyond our means.

We weren't missing out by a few thousand pounds either, but by *tens* of thousands, and it began to feel like we'd have to rent for longer or squeeze into a much smaller place. But we continued to scour websites, estate agent windows and local free-sheets, hoping our luck might change – and eventually it did.

What first seemed like a left-field, fairly unappealing find – to me at least – would eventually become an exceptional home, but that was hard to envisage when Rachel sent me a link to a three-bed, detached house on the outskirts of Woking. It looked charming enough on the outside, but the kids would have to share relatively small bedrooms while the interior was reminiscent of a design museum.

Only once we visited the small close where the property was located could I appreciate all the garden space at the front and back, plus an old, detached garage to one side that seemed ripe for demolition in order to make room for an extension. Or so Rachel thought.

Once inside, we were told it was a probate sale and the deceased owners had lived there since buying the newly constructed house in 1959. So much history, we mused, and it didn't appear there had been any major redecoration or modernisation over the following decades.

Still, Rachel believed the place had *potential* and so we decided to put in a cheeky offer, well below the asking price, which was still eye-wateringly high and way above anything I'd previously attempted to spend. Indeed, since being at Mum and Dad's, I'd never lived in anything larger than a terraced house. The scale of the work that would be required if we were successful was hard to comprehend, but Rachel had a little more experience in such matters and so we made our bid and waited to hear.

A fortnight on, by which time we'd already moved our sights to other targets, we received a surprise call with the news that our initial offer had just been accepted. I could scarcely believe it, with so much competition for everything else we'd seen, and quickly realised that having such a large bid accepted was even more intimidating than making it in the first place.

With no one living in the house, however, we didn't have long for the news to sink in and I was handed the keys on a frosty January morning a few weeks later. Minutes later, I unlocked and walked through the front door, alone, and my pulse quickened as I surveyed the cork-lined walls in the lounge, the polystyrene ceiling tiles upstairs and the shag-pile carpet in the hallway – all of which we now owned.

As one might expect in an unoccupied house in winter, the air was cold and musty, while the original furniture, all heralding from a similarly distant era, was still in its original place. Much of it reminded me of my grandparents' house and I felt like I'd boarded the *Marie Celeste* – time had seemingly stood still and, despite now owning the property, I questioned whether I had any right to be there.

I must confess, I even said a mental 'hello' to the previous occupiers – thanking them for letting me come into what had been their home for so long and promising I would continue to look after it. Whether that was a sign that my atheism was cracking, or that I was simply in a heightened emotional state and feeling sentimental, I don't know, but it seemed like the right thing to do.

Thankfully, I was soon joined by an experienced electrician and plumber, meaning there were multiple feet to disturb the dust and animated conversations to break the eerie silence. After a careful look round, the former of the experts told me that the house would need rewiring, especially if I was to get any insurance, while the plumber chuckled, shook his head and informed me he'd only seen a heating system like that once before – while he was training at college in the 1960s.

These jovial remarks formed my rude introduction to the financially draining world of renovating and extending something much bigger than a terraced house, although the real work wouldn't start until later in the year. Nor would I be joined by Rachel and her three kids until the spring, so I was to live there alone during the week, and with Fred at weekends, for the first few months.

I set about stripping the two main bedrooms as quickly as possible, before finding a plasterer and creating at least two havens of cleanliness and modernity for Fred and I to sleep in. My work was hampered by the fact I'd slipped a disc at the gym some weeks earlier, but I decided that dismantling built-in wardrobes and scraping tiles from ceilings was at least keeping me mobile – even if some weekends' efforts meant I could barely hobble to my new bed.

Soon after we all moved in, a momentous thing in itself, we had some plans drawn up and started looking for a builder. After several quotes, delays and endless questions, we chose a local man called Russ. His price was good, even if it was probably fifty per cent more than I would have paid in Sheffield, plus he had some satisfied customers we could visit nearby.

I also learned he was a fisherman, or used to be before business took over his life, and once we'd identified we were fellow anglers, albeit undergoing long periods of abstention, we shared pictures on our phones. His were mostly of a burly young man who was holding some huge carp and sporting an equally sizeable smile, who turned out to be one of Russ's sons. He was also a master bricklayer and so our shared passion became the foundation for many enjoyable chats throughout a long summer of groundwork.

The following nine months would prove to be turbulent, exciting and emotional in so many ways. There are far worse things to be endured, of course, but at one stage the lounge was our only usable space downstairs. It became our TV room, games room, a basic kitchen of sorts and our dining room. And after the ancient boiler packed up, it also became our only source of warmth – which came from an industrial heater that filled the place with a fiery glow and the smell of molten metal.

Scary electric bills, endless dust and the dodgy nutritional value of countless Pot Noodles might not have been so difficult to handle under normal circumstances, but we were a newly-forming family crammed into that chaotic space for several winter months. Each of us, adults and children, tried to comprehend the huge changes in our lives and, while I also have many happy memories from that time, I can't deny it was a period of continual adjustment, faith and patience.

When all of the noisy, expensive and tea-fuelled building work finally reached completion, I sent a final payment to Russ with the usual grimace, before saying a dazed but fond farewell to his team of tradespeople. Then we popped a cork or two and started to wonder how we'd ever fill the much larger house we'd created with enough stuff to stop it looking like an empty shell.

Rachel's parents and indeed my own folks had given us huge financial support by way of loans and they often reminded us that builders' quotes usually fall short of reality. However, no one had thought to point out they also don't include carpets, curtains, sofas or anything to hang on the many smooth walls that now surrounded us. Thankfully, we still had most of the original furniture and the retro pieces actually drew many admiring comments from our frequent visitors.

The first Monday morning to pass with no 7am knock at the door, or the usual round of hot drinks to make, brought a mixture of relief and sadness. Despite all the disruption and unexpected expenses, Russ had become part of our lives. He and his crew had delivered humour, friendship and tantalising progress, in addition to a fair bit of angst and frustration, on an almost daily basis. And he'd helped us achieve something significant, in a material sense, during a period when something else, less tangible but very special, had started to happen.

Despite the undoubted stress of creating a 'modern family' *and* a new home, all while doing a busy job and watching our money drain away at an alarming rate, it really started to feel worth it. I had to sell my old terraced house in Sheffield to get us over the line, but we now owned a property that comfortably accommodated everyone, along with a garage to store bikes, tools, half-empty tins of paint – and my almost-forgotten fishing tackle.

It still didn't get any use, or not beyond the DWSSC matches, for a couple more years either. I was still commuting to north London and putting in long hours when the extension was finished, while Rachel worked part-time and was kept just as busy with a packed calendar of parents' evenings, children's football matches and other sporting commitments. We still had lots of fun along the way and our relationship proved more than a match for all the upheaval, but our time was largely devoted to working and helping the kids settle into their new lives.

Despite some inevitable ups and downs, they were quick to adapt and became closer with every passing weekend they were able to spend together. Watching films and drinking hot chocolate while squeezed onto the 1960s sofa became a popular pastime, particularly during winter months, while inventing new games to play on a giant trampoline (a gift from their combined grandparents) was a big draw in the summertime.

The trampoline was located in our back garden – the first patch of ground I'd owned that couldn't be covered in three or four strides – and that was another reason that my carp gear, and anything else I didn't take on the matches, continued to be ignored. Over many grimy and exhausting weekends, I ripped out numerous overgrown laurels, gathered up stones and old roots and then re-seeded the soil with grass.

We needed somewhere fit for kick-abouts, chases and a waterslide made from plastic sheeting. Even if that meant filling in a tiny garden pond because of where it was located – although not before Fraser, the eldest, had managed to fall into it one evening. Before it was emptied completely, I also remember that Lara and I rescued a surprising number of newts, before taking them to a new home in a nearby park.

Life continued in this hectic but loving, entertaining and rewarding way – with endless 'firsts' experienced as a co-habiting couple and still-forming family along the way – before another pair of significant events conspired to shake things up again. The first was somewhat in my control and probably should have been less testing under normal circumstances, while the other took lots of people, including myself, by surprise.

At the beginning of our second year in our new home I was offered the chance to leave the role I'd been in for nearly a decade. Now that may sound more like a disaster than an opportunity to most, but this was a company I'd helped to create and then devoted much of my time to. I had been there from its creation to international expansion, and then from near-collapse to an equally demanding turnaround effort during the previous eighteen months.

The option to leave in an orderly manner, with six months' notice and some final projects to complete, followed by a further six months of 'garden leave', which I could use to find my next job, therefore came as a welcome way to make a much-needed move – all while protecting the income needed by two households. It was a generous arrangement the chairman of the firm was willing to offer due to the proverbial blood, sweat and tears I'd given over the years, so I took him up on the offer before starting to hunt for a new employer.

I felt determined to prove myself in a bigger company again and events unfolded remarkably well to begin with. After a few months of intensive 'networking' in London, I got wind of a senior communications role with one of the smaller, but ambitious and growing banks. Several interviews followed, including a positive meeting with the chief executive, and I was reassured there would soon be a concrete offer on the table, just a few weeks after saying an emotional farewell to my previous firm.

Yet before the promised contract could arrive, everything fell through and my carefully considered plan lay in tatters. I'd enjoyed a week or two of no emails, no early alarms, no commuter trains or long days in the office, when I woke one morning to hear some unexpected news. I read with dismay that the British people had voted to leave the European Union. Brexit was born and, although my initial reaction was one of sadness and disappointment, it quickly turned to dread as the company in question informed me that they were pausing all new hires. Indefinitely.

Not only was my hard-won job offer withdrawn, but every specialist recruiter I'd met over the preceding months also told me their clients were now paralysed by uncertainty. Again, there are far more difficult hardships to be endured, but having made the decision to leave my previous employer and with two families depending on my salary, my guts gradually tightened into a sickening knot.

I still had some time on my hands, but no one had any new leads to offer and I found myself, mentally at least, in a lonely place filled with worry and doubt. With six months of salary payments remaining, I realised I needed to start from scratch and find something that would cover all of my outgoings in a niche job market that was now as frigid as the Trent in February.

What's more, if I failed to secure something

substantial before the end of my agreed garden leave, I would be unemployed just in time for Christmas. We were facing the possibility that we might even need to sell the house we'd just worked so hard to turn into a home, but I slowly came to terms with the situation and organised as many coffee meetings in the capital as I could, while scouring job pages and LinkedIn for any sign of something suitable.

Life again felt more complicated than I'd ever imagined it could be throughout my childhood and early adult years. Although Granddad would no doubt have reminded me, "worse things 'appen at sea," coming relatively soon after the upheaval of divorce, falling in love and forming a new family, the fresh responsibility of seeking employment weighed heavily on my shoulders.

Despite the fact the new fishing season was only a few weeks old – and I'd naturally been anticipating a glut of opportunities to wet a line before starting a new job – my rods seemed destined to remain in the garage, unbent and unloved. Instead of enjoying the only break from work I'd ever managed to engineer, I was spending yet more hours in front of a computer screen and cursing my luck.

Yet it seems some clouds *do* have a silver lining, because it eventually became apparent that there's only so much job-hunting and networking one can do in such a narrow field as mine. Once I'd sent all the emails or dialled all the numbers I could generate each day, it became a waiting game – so I eventually realised the most effective approach was focusing my efforts during the first half of the day and then trying to relax, knowing I'd done what I could, in the afternoons and evenings.

Aside from the ever-present background worry, it was a glorious summer of blue skies and little rain and, after

The Magic of Fishing

beavering away on a keyboard all morning, I started to enjoy the newfound time at home. I sometimes laid on a towel in the garden and soaked up some rays for a few hours, while listening to music or reading a book. And around the end of July, I picked up my copy of *Casting at the Sun* by Chris Yates.

I hadn't read it for years but immediately found myself immersed in his captivating tales again, before moving swiftly on to another of his books. And during those first few afternoons of guilt-free leisure time, I felt the load of my unemployed status lift a little. I regularly enthused about my welcome new source of distraction and inspiration – so much, in fact, that Rachel eventually questioned why I didn't actually stop talking about it and *go* fishing.

The seed was sown and less than a week later her nudge led to something I can confidently describe as life-changing. The initial concern I felt about the idea of disappearing off to the water, when there was so much still at stake, was soon eroded by the powerful literary current of Chris Yates' writing. Just as escaping to Africa had saved me from some kind of breakdown a few years before, I began to reason that I might be more effective if I could find a way to cope with the pressure I'd put myself under.

My favourite fishing author not only helped me escape from reality for an hour or two each day, but within his stories I also found instructions for how I should reconnect with my almost-dormant passion. They were not the precise directions of a technical manual, but the gentle guidance of poetic love letters written to the ponds, lakes and rivers he'd fished. His words stirred my imagination and sent my mind's eye wandering along the banks of the local River Wey – banks that I hadn't visited for an age.

Yates' disdain for modern tackle, methods and baits – more than matched by his enthusiasm for simplicity, enjoyment and the art of trying to catch fish of all shapes and sizes – was infectious. So much so that I began to wonder if my own approach to angling had become too complicated. So complicated that it sometimes felt too much effort to go.

Surely something was wrong, I reasoned, and I began to hatch a plan that would allow me to prove the theory while summer was still in full swing. I decided I should imitate the author's decluttered approach, and the following afternoon I stopped hunting for jobs and began searching for suitable tackle for an experimental outing.

No carbon pole would be required, nor electronic bite alarms, bags of pellets or a trolley to haul a mountain of gear from the car park of some commercial fishery. Instead, I hoped to recreate the buzz I'd felt when first exploring the rivers around Woking and, even more importantly, I wanted to try and catch anything that might show an interest in my bait. My first trip would not be about trying to catch the biggest fish, or the biggest combined weight of fish, but whether I could feel the old magic again.

With that rather lofty goal in mind, I located a light quiver tip rod and paired it with a small Mitchell reel loaded with four-pound line. Next I emptied one of my plastic boxes that had been filled with old carp tackle and replaced the heavy weights, Teflon-coated hooks and technical rig components with a few floats, a tub of split-shot, a disgorger and some packets of smaller hooks.

I had so much tackle to choose from within the garage, but for once I wasn't torn between the numerous options. My principle was ruthlessly simple – I would only take a similar amount of terminal tackle that I'd once carried around in my cherished cigar box.

A landing net, some food, drink and my club membership book were soon added to the modest pile and then I spent a few minutes digging around in the compost heap for a handful of worms. They seemed like a fitting bait for such a stripped-back session – being free, natural and appealing to every freshwater fish – and reminding myself of that fact helped build my confidence as I drove to the river.

It had taken less than thirty minutes to get on my way and I felt a swell of anticipation as I turned off a busy slip road and onto an unassuming country lane. All the other drivers accelerated onwards, eager to reach the dual carriageway ahead, but my route was quiet and calm. The road soon narrowed to a single track and then came to an end before a cluster of stunning properties that had undoubtedly stood around the central mill pool for hundreds of years.

Parking in a layby, I was soon out of the car and, with so little to carry, easily negotiating a stile and making my way along a woodland path. Enjoying the dappled shade, birdsong and knowledge I would be at the river within five minutes, I was hit by continual waves of nostalgia. Not only for my previous walks down the same path – a good few years earlier, when I was a younger man with far fewer concerns or responsibilities – but also for my relationship with fishing in general.

Walking alone among the trees, sending pigeons clattering from branches or squirrels racing up trunks as I went, I felt like I could've been any age. I was almost overwhelmed by a dizzying kaleidoscope of memories, emotions and thoughts. On the one hand I felt giddy, like a matchday morning at Downing Road, yet also calmed by the familiarity of the surroundings. And I marvelled at how the simple fact I was carrying fishing tackle transformed the experience of following a fairly unremarkable track.

Eventually I glimpsed the narrow, overgrown and reed-fringed river and a few moments later I was on its grassy bank once more. It was perhaps seven or eight years since I'd last stood in that spot and the moment of return had a dreamlike quality as I contemplated how much water had passed under the bridge – both a metaphorical one and the literal one just downstream from where I'd paused.

Tears suddenly stung my eyes and a lump rose in my throat that would have rendered me mute if a fellow angler had happened to stumble upon me right then. I wiped my cheeks with the back of my hand and sucked in a few deep breaths. If anyone had been by my side I couldn't have articulated what I was feeling or why my emotions were so high, but looking back it was the realisation I'd spent far too long away from something I loved.

So long, it seemed, that I had almost forgotten about it. Only by revisiting a once-familiar haunt, alone and removed from modern life, had a lifetime of memories, associations and feelings been unleashed. Feeling lightheaded, I knew the only cure was to find a likely-looking spot and then try to reconnect with this place, my hobby and – hopefully – some fish.

I didn't have to explore far and soon found a patch of worn earth with thick undergrowth on either side and a short, steep slope behind. It looked like a natural cocoon and, having slid down into the shade and quietly unloaded my gear by the water's edge, I looked over the swirling surface in front of me and knew it was right.

The way my fingers trembled as I prepared to fish was also familiar and I began humming to myself with a growing sense of contentment. As I sat on my folding chair, bent forward and focused on tackling up, the August sun moved far enough for its rays to pass the bushes on my left and warm my back. And by the time I was ready to bait my hook I was feeling *joyous*.

There was no fancy rig, only a few split-shot on a loop of nylon, forming a 'link-ledger' that I calculated would just hold bottom in the slack to my right. I didn't intend to use any special bait either, just one of the lively worms I'd dug up an hour or two earlier. Once hooked, I gently swung it away from me and then lowered it into the water a few feet from the bank downstream.

I placed the rod on the ground, not even bothering with a rest, and watched the gentle flow take up the slack in my line before pulling the quiver tip into a barely discernible curve. I brushed my hands together and prepared to wait, hunting around for the can of drink I'd packed and telling myself this short trip would still end gloriously even if I didn't get a single bite.

I didn't get to prove that bet right, however, as a few minutes later there came a couple of sharp plucks on the tip, sparking the kind of adrenaline shot I hadn't felt for some time. My right hand moved instinctively, hovering just above the rod, while my breathing unconsciously paused.

This was what I had been missing, I thought, and moments later there came a savage pull. The sight was electrifying, jerking me into action and a rather rusty strike. There followed a steady jag-jag-jag, as a fish bolted from the bank and into the main flow.

I had hardly dared hope for a bite, let alone to connect with something on my first cast, and my delight only grew as I realised it was no tiddler. It wasn't anything special, either, but I grinned like an idiot while carefully playing the fish towards me and realised I might even need the landing net.

Up came a handsome perch, less than a pound in weight but looking magnificent in its striped chainmail. It shook its head before making a last attempt to evade capture and I almost laughed out loud, such was the pleasure of seeing it.

Gentle pressure brought it to the surface once more, before I was able to net it and claim my prize. Once unhooked, I actually thanked it out loud for gracing my day. Not that it would have welcomed our brief encounter but as I slipped it back, no worse for wear, I knew it was one of the most important catches of my life.

CHAPTER 21

The Next Generation

If I had to place a wager on whether Fred, Fraser, Lara or Ewan will become keen anglers, I would have to guess no. Fred was naturally my first hope for an heir to my fishing crown and, since that special hour we shared on the canal, he's accompanied me on several lengthier trips and enjoyed them to varying degrees.

He even took part in a DWSSC match a few years ago, although he probably savoured the huge breakfast and friendly attention from his fellow competitors more than six hours of concerted angling, or indeed the continual coaching from me. He definitely had the skills to compete, finishing in the top half of the weights despite frequently requesting snack breaks, but he didn't exactly beg to attend the next one.

He always enjoyed catching a few fish and spending time with me as a young boy, but never showed the intense interest that gripped me from an early age. So perhaps I've just disproven something I stated earlier – that you either get it or you don't – and my son's an example of someone who can feel a touch of intrigue while never falling head over heels in love.

Still, whatever the mysterious influences of DNA and upbringing – nature or nurture, as they say – my hopes of *changing* Fred into a fellow fishing fanatic were possibly doomed from the off. And they certainly received a hammer-blow during a father-and-son visit to a picturesque pond last summer.

It's a lovely little venue near Dorking and, although not much bigger than The Pond at Moorwood Lane, it's home to countless small and ravenous carp. I often head there towards the end of winter, when I'm keen to feel a bend in my rod again, so I calculated it would also give my lad a rush if we could hook one or two fish at close quarters. Let him feel the exhilarating first run, with a bow wave heading out towards the middle of the shallow pool, I reasoned, and that would surely fan his barely smouldering embers of interest.

I'd never failed to catch fewer than five or six of those mini fighting machines on previous visits and reaching double figures wasn't uncommon, even during short evenings, so I had every confidence in my strategy. I therefore spent most of the twenty-minute drive over the Surrey Hills describing how the speed and strength of our intended quarry would take his breath away.

Aside from being an excellent rugby player, occasional tennis enthusiast and dedicated online gamer, Fred's been raised with impeccable manners and good emotional intelligence, so he tried to show some enthusiasm in return – humouring my excitement with a few questions and glimmers of anticipation. And he also sat patiently once we'd arrived, walked to our swim and started to tackle up.

Before doing so, I scattered some grains of sweetcorn in the margin to our right and soon felt reassured by the usual tell-tale signs of activity. I noticed an occasional shudder from nearby reeds, obviously disturbed by the passing of a sizeable flank, followed by a few vortexes on the surface which betrayed the upturned tail strokes of feeding fish.

I explained the positive indications to Fred, who seemed only half-interested, but I could already picture their feeding mouths, preoccupied by the free offerings. I felt certain this would be the trip when he finally caught the bug, or at least caught a few carp. And, to my mind, the two were becoming inextricably linked. Surely, I thought, if he could replicate the kind of multiple captures I'd enjoyed several times before, then a longer-term fascination would follow.

I even wondered if I'd tried to introduce him to my passion too gently, or even too traditionally, because today's kids seem to need instant gratification and thrills. Just like the all-action video games that can hold Fred's attention until the moment they're switched off, I felt this was a chance to provide the angling equivalent. Soon he'd be getting quick bites, plenty of them and hard scraps from fish that could take a good five or ten minutes to subdue.

The sun was already dipping below the narrow strip of trees behind us, but it was still warm enough for shorts and T-shirts and the air was filled with gentle summer scents that reminded me of so many other evening sessions when bigger fish had become that little bit less wary – and therefore catchable. Everything felt right for making some indelible memories with my son and, feeling buoyed by the prospect, I promised we'd stop at a pub on the way home.

I was confident we could catch a few fish in only an hour or two, well before darkness fell, and was in no rush to make the first cast. We therefore took our time getting comfortable in two folding chairs and only once I'd patiently reminded him how to set up a float rig did we bait the hook with two yellow grains. I then helped him lower them into position beside the bed of reeds where I'd already seen so many signs of feeding fish.

The float settled and I flicked a few more freebies around it, telling Fred to keep hold of the cork handle and be ready to strike at any moment. He's generally good at following instructions and did as I asked for fifteen minutes, before I began to wonder if our bait had landed in a snag or perhaps been covered by weed. We checked, to be safe, and all seemed fine – so we repeated the earlier process before settling back down to wait again.

Fred continued to humour my strong sense of anticipation, along with regular reassurances that 'something was about to happen' and it was only after a full hour had passed that he began to get a bit fed up. In fact, he sighed audibly and dejectedly as I whispered, "Any second, Fred, any second!" for the third or fourth time. And what's more, I couldn't blame him.

I don't wish anyone to endure a written version of our unfortunate experience that evening, or not in any detail, but suffice to say we didn't hook or land a single fish. And I still can't explain why. Yes, he missed a handful of bites due to inexperience, but they were few and far between. What seemed like a nailed-on opportunity for him to catch something a bit more exhilarating just would *not* materialise – no matter how hard I willed it to.

I'm a stubborn bugger, so only after another hour of persistent encouragement, bewildering inactivity and increasing frustration did Fred put us both out of our misery. One might say he put a bitter cherry on top of my rapidly deflating cake, by uttering the immortal words: "Dad, this is really boring, so can we please go home?"

He emphasised two words – 'boring' and 'please' – and I realised my dreams of an angling heir lay in tatters. Not only that, but in one short evening I'd driven him to plead for mercy. So, finally resigned to failure, we did indeed pack up shortly after his innocent and completely understandable confession. And as I lifted the gear back onto my shoulders in the growing gloom, I not only cursed our luck but knew my son hadn't inherited his father's natural affinity with water.

I couldn't blame him for that, or for getting frustrated, either. Especially not after the build-up I'd given him. But it was his lack of interest in the little things – which still got my own heart pumping – that spoke truth to me. When I saw our float dip briefly, shortly after a few bubbles had been sent up, I talked through gritted teeth and pictured the imminent moment when Fred would connect with something unseen and unstoppable, but to him it was just a nibble. It wasn't a proper bite, a hooked fish or anything tangible.

I have no doubt he can enjoy fishing for short periods and has done so since, including a recent and more productive visit to the same pond, along with Lara, his step-sister. And I believe we'll have more fun times together on the bank, but at the end of that fateful trip I was forced to compare his growing boredom with the joyful enthusiasm he displays when doing something he *really* enjoys, like watching a funny film or going on a rollercoaster.

While reloading the car, I mused that perhaps it, whatever 'it' may be, skips a generation, as it seemingly had with my own dad. But I'd already come to terms with the realisation that Fred simply enjoys other things in life, just like most of my family and friends. I still made a silent curse on the pool and its freakishly uncooperative inhabitants as we drove away, but was chuckling to myself by the time we sat down in the pub shortly afterwards.

One of the strangest things about that visit to Frog Island, as it's known, is that I've since returned a number of times and the fishing's always been as good as usual. Lara's been there a couple of times, too, and she has demonstrated some innate interest and skill. Indeed, she showed some promise right from our first trip together, which was to a local club water a few years ago.

I can still picture her clearly that evening without the need to look at my photos – unbearably cute in denim dungarees, her white-blonde hair tied up in a ponytail and sitting patiently on the wooden fishing platform like Huckleberry Finn. Lara is as much substance as she is style, however, and within minutes of showing her how to set up a similar float rig to one Fred first used on the canal, she was at least *partially* hooked.

Fascinated by my collection of floats and other bits of tackle, she nodded at each stage of our preparations before insisting on hooking the maggots for herself. Then she was soon striking at bites with a natural grace and determination – even unhooking the fish she caught and showing none of the apprehension the boys had. Just as a young Fred was quick to handle a rugby ball and shrug off attempted tackles, Lara seemed to grasp the basics of fishing without much effort.

She was enthralled by the small roach, rudd and perch she caught during the hour or two we had there – studying them carefully before releasing them with the same kind of reverence I'd always shown my catches. And perhaps the biggest hint she felt a real connection, or certainly a little more than the other kids, came when she asked for "one more cast" when I decided it was getting too dark.

As she reasoned for a bit longer by the water, I was struck by a vivid memory of my own pleading with Granddad and couldn't resist letting her have a few more goes. The extra minutes ensured she landed that official 'final fish' which most anglers like to finish with, especially at the end of a decent pleasure session.

Then we did eventually pack up, before stopping at a pub on the way home. I remember we returned to the car, after two Cokes and some peanuts, to find a bright-green grasshopper on the windscreen. Incredibly, it stayed there, somehow clinging to the glass at up to fifty miles per hour all the way back, which allowed Lara to examine it more closely once we got home.

Fraser, the eldest, enjoyed a similar trip to the same pond and also showed some ability, perhaps with a touch less excitement but some clear enjoyment, nonetheless. Like the others, he is talented and interested in many other things – from football and tennis, to music and films – so without the time to take him fishing on a regular basis, it's difficult to see him following in my wader-clad footsteps either. Especially now he's a good-looking teenager and on the brink of discovering the joys of young adulthood.

Given more time, or specifically more of *my* time, who knows, but I sense he will be happy and successful in life without sharing that particular passion. Lara, and occasionally Fred, have made the only *requests* to go fishing and Ewan is yet to try it properly, but then he finds sitting still for more than five minutes quite difficult. Certainly if it doesn't involve a digital screen or the eating of food to maintain his batteries.

He's the charming, cheeky and playful youngest sibling – a bundle of energy who loves to run around a football pitch for ninety minutes but doesn't 'see the point' of an hour's stroll in the countryside. I recall talking to him gently one afternoon, to explain that I was taking Fred and Lara fishing again, but, if he fancied it, his time would come soon. He looked at me quizzically, as if I was joking, and got straight back to YouTube.

The one fishing-related spark I've seen in him was when he and his siblings came to visit me on the river on a recent summer's evening, and he was fascinated by a large eel I'd caught. He was happy to wrestle with it for a picture, which is more than most fishermuggles would dare. But of course I don't hold his lack of interest against him – or anyone for that matter – I only wish I could share the magic.

While I can see Fred and Lara genuinely enjoying more time chasing fish with me over the coming years, I don't believe any of them will end up going on their own steam. I've been known to be wrong, on rare occasions, but it seems I may have to wait for another generation to arrive. Or keep trying with some of my younger nieces and nephews, which is tricky from 180 miles away but still enjoyable once or twice a year.

Screens, whether of the phone, tablet or TV variety, are one of the things that wind me up these days and, while it makes me sound like a grumpy old man, I'm sure they're to blame for a weakening interest in the natural world. Some kids appear to be incapable of devising their own entertainment using imagination alone and they even watch videos of other people playing games on, you guessed it, other screens.

I struggle to understand that particular trend, although perhaps I'm a bit of a hypocrite because I was an avid gamer, on a Sega Mega Drive, during my teenage years. I also spend most of my working days looking at screens of one kind or another and enjoy watching films or Netflix series with Rachel during the darker evenings, so who am I to criticise? I just despair at the semi-permanent bent necks, the glazed eyes and selectively deaf ears – particularly on bright weekend mornings in summer, when I'd love to be walking towards the river with the sun on my back and the smell of clover in my nostrils.

Fred's just entered his teenage years and he's a screen-addict too, but he's also handsome, strong and already above my shoulder. He's a fine specimen of a son who I'm actually very proud of most of the time, just like my lovely step-children. I'm glad we have been fishing together and, despite their general preference for other pastimes, they may now have *some* appreciation of my strange obsession.

I'm also proud that Fred's mum and I get on so well; still sharing delight in our son's achievements and activities, whether it's his talent for rugby, a parents' evening at school or a birthday party with his friends. In fact, all the kids have adapted well to being part of a modern family and, although there's been so much change and the odd difficult moment, they're now closer than ever.

I believe Rachel and I have not only found enduring love together, but created a caring, hectic and fun-filled family home – a place that feels full of life whether it's just the two of us, enjoying a quiet, romantic weekend, or all six people arguing at the dinner table. Although they're few and far between, it seems there are some things in life more important than fishing.

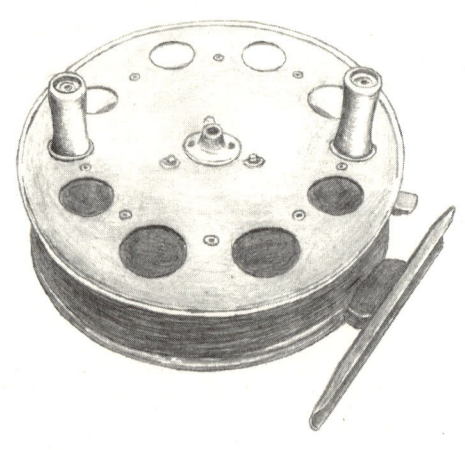

CHAPTER 22

Simple Pleasures

Writing so sporadically, usually in snatched hours between the demands of middle-aged work and family life, it's taken far longer than I expected to recount some of the cherished memories that fishing has given me. Despite an early rush of determined productivity, a few years have passed since I began to type – and making that start was only possible after taking my first career break in more than two decades.

The initial few months of largely unplanned, unstructured days were not without pressure, worry or concerted effort to find employment, but I gained precious breathing space from the rat race and, almost unexpectedly, fell back under a powerful spell that was first cast beside a tiny farm pond in the late 1970s.

Not that I'd ever wanted, planned or indeed fully managed to escape the magnetic pull of lakes, rivers and canals, but the strength of my devotion had undeniably waned over the hectic, sometimes stressful years leading up to that precious time off. While re-reading some classic books about my hobby was enough to begin with, I was soon inspired to spend more time actually doing it – and it was the newfound freedom to immerse myself in something I loved that fuelled my creative fire too.

Being back on the bank a few times a week, both on familiar and virgin waters, provoked so many happy flashbacks, while somehow making them more *real* too. It felt like I'd taken a collection of faded, black-and-white prints and somehow converted them into full-colour, high-definition digital images.

The really productive, action-packed fishing sessions on scorching afternoons left me satisfied, slimy and tired out, while the quiet ones afforded me solitude and peace in which to think, reminisce and recuperate. All my senses were stimulated and I was reminded of the simple pleasures in life, along with the importance of family, friends and the infinite wonders of nature.

Yet not long after that significant and emotional period of change – when emails, business meetings and financial worries were replaced, or at least soothed, by the sight of swans, kingfishers, damselflies and grass snakes – I inevitably had to re-join the world of work. And despite enjoying many aspects of leadership and being back in business as part of a team, plus the immense relief of finding financial security, spare time inevitably became a rare commodity again.

Fishing, whether attempting a short trip or continuing to write about it, became more challenging too. I was back to reality: starting a senior role in a company with around 30,000 people and millions of customers, so my daydreams of big fish were again stifled by bustling offices, endless messages and significant problems to solve.

Joining an unfamiliar industry was also a shock to the system, like going back to school after a long summer break. The first year was daunting, draining and a little chaotic as I tried to absorb a seemingly endless stream of new information and make tentative connections with a vast number of people. Being back at work meant security – but at a cost, including the fact I couldn't seem to complete something I first hoped to achieve in a matter of months.

My stories may have remained unfinished for many years to come, too. Perhaps until the end of my career, when I'd be old enough to add many more chapters if I could only stand the sight of a laptop. Now, however, things are about to change again and not through my own choosing. While I don't believe in destiny, life is full of unexpected twists and some of them can feel quite fateful – which was certainly the case when I received a call from the CEO of my current company, with some bad news.

Over the preceding months I'd continued working hard and enjoying time with my family, meaning that writing the final chapters had begun to feel near-impossible or, worse still, unimportant. As another winter began to relinquish its grip, I started to believe I'd missed my only real chance of finishing my ode to angling – back when finding another job was the only major distraction and the long summer days seemed to stretch forever.

Life had now been back in a familiar, largely predictable groove for a few years and, other than my inability to finish what I started, there could be few complaints. But then the world began to shift, and shift for good. Along came a seismic event on a global scale that, initially at least, extinguished any lingering thoughts of writing about or indeed going fishing.

Towards the end of 2019, the same year I married Rachel, reports of a new virus called COVID-19 began to emerge from China and a procession of concerned scientists explained how it was not only transmitting easily amongst humans, but some unfortunate people were developing severe and sometimes fatal symptoms. Despite these dire warnings and unsettling footage of Wuhan hospitals that looked more like makeshift medical facilities in a warzone, life in Europe continued in a semi-normal fashion for a short while longer.

At least until another epicentre was identified in northern Italy, early in 2020. And just a few weeks later the UK joined every other nation in the ongoing battle against a disease that had already claimed hundreds of thousands of lives and begun to break local and global economies. By spring, aside from NHS staff and other key workers who had little choice but to continue delivering essential services, the population was in full lockdown – confined to our homes for all but the most pressing emergencies.

Many, including Rachel and I, were suddenly working from home while trying to home-school, or at least prevent a mutiny amongst, the children. We took breaks around 5pm to watch the daily government briefings, with a growing sense of disbelief, while sometimes getting our allowed half-hour of exercise later in the evening with a walk or bike ride around the local common.

We used video calls to stay in touch with colleagues, family and friends, and grew increasingly familiar with terms like 'the R number', 'furloughing' and 'social distancing'. As we tried to digest the alarming international updates on the numbers of lives lost to COVID-19, we clapped for the NHS every Thursday evening, looked out for our neighbours via WhatsApp and found new – or sometimes old – forms of entertainment for the kids.

Every day I felt extremely thankful and somewhat bemused that none of my family, friends or colleagues had been seriously affected, at least not in terms of their physical wellbeing. That is still the most important, personal fact of the past few months. Yet, as one of the leaders of a major company that was adjusting to the crisis and trying hard to look after the safety and needs of both employees and customers, it became increasingly clear the pandemic would have all kinds of serious ramifications.

It was already dramatically affecting industries like travel, hospitality and entertainment, while countless small businesses were forced to close and millions of people's existing livelihoods were either threatened, suspended or ended. Indeed, some experts began to predict that far more lives would ultimately be impacted or potentially lost due to the virus's long-term economic consequences.

Although fortunate enough to avoid the illness amongst any close family or friends, the financial ramifications of the pandemic began to feel less theoretical by the week. I sensed difficult times just over the horizon and – after participating in many emotional and protracted management discussions about the future of the workforce, maintaining financial stability and potential threats to the company – I was informed of my own redundancy towards the end of May.

Despite everything we still had to be thankful for, it was a visceral moment and something I'm still coming to terms with while typing these words. I'm an optimist – or at least a stubborn pragmatist – by nature, and keep reminding myself that health, family and friends are more important than money. Yet suddenly facing the prospect of worrying about mortgage payments and bills again, combined with an arduous search for another senior role in a half-frozen job market, keeps me awake at night.

Recollections of the mounting pressure, nagging doubts and, ultimately, the lone responsibility of finding a new role just three or four years ago are still fresh. So fresh in fact they've started swirling around in my dreams or suddenly making my stomach flip during the daylight hours.

I've had to make some loyal, hard-working and talented people redundant over recent years and sitting on either side of that table is an unpleasant experience, but now it's my turn to feel rejected. My turn to wonder if I could've done anything differently, to tell myself it's 'just business' and to try and stay calm in front of the kids.

I need to keep the lurking panic at bay and remain grateful for everything I still have. Like a lovely family; genuine, caring friends; a garden big enough for me and the kids to have recently dug a pond in; and one of the sunniest, hottest springs on record.

I'll be placed on garden leave soon, for only the second time in my life, and while I continue to carry out my professional duties until then, I cannot help but be struck by the timing of my exit. Much like the last time I was searching for something new – albeit through my own, calculated choice – I will shortly leave my lockdown workstation in the lounge, with its well-worn keyboard and continually vibrating phone, just as a new fishing season begins.

Fishing is one of the few pastimes allowed to restart, as the beleaguered government begins to tentatively ease some restrictions, and I naturally took advantage of the new exemption right away, enjoying some brief but fruitful trips over the first two weekends. With the traditional season still closed and my local club waters off-limits, I opted for a couple of nearby commercial fisheries. They attracted hordes of other eager anglers, like moths to a flame, but it was still a fantastic feeling to be there.

As I cautiously joined their ranks and made my first few casts, I revelled in the sudden access to fresh air with no time limits, the relatively natural scenery and the capture of a few unwitting carp. Like any significant change, however, this new freedom took some getting used to and, while I was happy just to wet a line, by the time I finished my third outing to a manmade, heavily stocked pond, my enjoyment was accompanied by a growing desire to find somewhere with more peace, solitude and wildlife.

The river was calling me again and now I only have a week or two to wait. Not only that, but aside from spending time with my family, a few household chores to complete – oh, and the unavoidable need to find another job – I will have all the time in the world. More time to walk back along familiar paths, to pause and assess the conditions, pick a spot and then flick out a bait to see what might be biting. And once the old spell's embraced me with all its force, then maybe, just maybe, I'll complete this book.

I resisted the urge to write about angling for so long, then couldn't find time to finish doing it, but now it's close to completion it feels like fate has intervened again. If I can use some of the time gained from my redundancy to finish these stories, then someday I may even be partly thankful for losing that job when I did. Perhaps I'll be able to look back at these unbelievable, uncertain times and know that at least I finished trying to explain what makes fishing so special to me.

I've always been sentimental and sometimes dwell on life's milestones too much, such as the fact I will turn fifty in a few years. Like most adults of a certain age, I find it incomprehensible that I'm no longer in the prime of youth or that one of my nieces has recently become the first Moorwood to attend Oxford University.

I'm noticing the crow's feet growing around my eyes – no doubt deepened by summer days spent squinting against the sun's glare, trying to watch the tip of a distant float – or the fact my hair's rapidly greying and I'm increasingly susceptible to back trouble. How can it be, I wonder, that three out of the four children under our roof are now teenagers, while my parents have a dozen grandchildren to keep them busy and I sometimes find myself worrying about my lack of a decent pension?

It's amazing what can happen in the blink of an eye, but at least I'm still a 'young'un' in the eyes of my fellow DWSSC members. And, as my grandparents taught me, no matter how old you are, it's always possible to get older. In other words, be grateful for what you have – because if you reach a hundred or even beyond, as one of Rachel's grandmothers did, you'll think people in their nineties are relatively young and be positively envious of eighty-somethings.

So, despite my indignation that time does indeed seem to speed up as you get older, I'm also aware that I have many things to appreciate and celebrate. Including the never-ending joy of trying to catch fish. Despite being a busy husband, father, son and brother, fishing still is and always will be a precious part of my life.

Since rekindling the love affair during my previous career break, I've continued to keep things *simple*, which I urge any busy, semi-retired or new anglers to try, because it's helped me appreciate any rare time spent by the water even more. I still journey northwards four or five times every year – meeting up with Andy, Harry, John, Dennis, Mick, Simon and the rest of the club for the summer matches – and I still do well in them, too, although they're really more about friendship and enjoyment of course.

These long-running pilgrimages to my hometown still give me a chance to reconnect with a simpler, slower era – leaving the frenetic, digital distractions of modern life behind and embracing adored traditions once more. After a three- or four-hour drive (if the traffic's good), any remaining work worries, pressures or mental to-do lists soon disperse when I stop off at a large tackle shop in Dronfield Woodhouse.

It always makes for a perfect break in the journey, with the worst of the miles already done and a chance to lose myself in an Aladdin's cave of fishing treasures. Entering the sprawling building to hear the dry wit of locals now officially signals the beginning of another match weekend – and once I'm stocked up with bait and a few unplanned extras, it's only another twenty minutes' drive to my parents' house.

Aside from seeing my family and familiar places, the summer matches are my strongest remaining link to a more carefree time of life. Not that I don't like who and where I am right now, of course, but each trip provides a reliable, if lengthening, time-tunnel to an incredibly special childhood.

Although my desire to catch as many fish as possible hasn't faded, matchdays have little to do with wanting to beat the men on either side of me. I simply want to prove to myself that, despite a distinct lack of practice, I've *still* got the experience, knowledge and skills to make the most of whichever peg I draw.

I usually still buy *The Angling Times* and *Angler's Mail* on my way northwards, too, albeit from a service station rather than a cosy newsagent's shop on the outskirts of the city. Later, just before sleep, I can then read about the more 'serious' match results from around the country, some with sponsorships and prize money worth tens or even hundreds of thousands of pounds, or check out the latest gear being launched.

There's always plenty of new tackle reviewed or advertised in these magazines and I often marvel at the choice, or sometimes the cost, of what's now available to contemporary anglers. Take some of the latest seat boxes – the 21st-century equivalent of a 1970s wicker basket, constructed of carbon fibre and aluminium – which can be acquired for anything up to £2,000. It's an eye-watering price tag that would've shocked Granddad, and doubtless he'd have pointed out that they weigh a lot more than his old basket too.

Not that I'm against technical progress. Nor am I innocent of making some extravagant purchases over the years but, certainly while I'm working, my carp tackle still gathers dust in the garage and my match gear rarely gets used beyond the trips to Sheffield. Nowadays, the things I reach for most frequently are a folding canvas chair, a multi-pocketed shoulder bag and a narrow 'quiver' containing a handful of rods and a landing net handle.

Collectively, I think of these modest items as my 'river outfit', which is designed to be as compact and lightweight as possible. That way, it can be quickly thrown into the car at short notice and then easily carried to just about anywhere I fancy. I'm lucky – or have worked hard enough – to own so much tackle that I can now separate it into different categories, and indeed to have enough space to store it all, but being realistic about the kind of fishing I can achieve has changed my relationship with my hobby for the better.

A simpler approach has allowed me to replicate that memorable session on the Wey – when I arrived at the river after a long absence and felt the electricity return so strongly – many times since. Not in terms of the overwhelming emotions of that trip, but more an ability to immerse myself in nature for a few hours and enjoy trying to tempt whatever may bite.

Despite often being limited to short sessions, my pared-back and generalist approach has allowed me to revisit many old haunts with renewed enthusiasm and also explore new stretches – some of which have proven surprisingly productive. Roving around and trying a few lengths of the river across different months and seasons has been inspiring, and I'm now liable to agree with the increasing sentiment that at least some of our natural fish stocks have never been in such good health.

Long before the pandemic reared its ugly head, there were many serious challenges and ongoing threats to our waterways, ecosystems and wildlife. They include other diseases, predation by non-native species, pollution and other forms of environmental damage – and that's before factoring in the global climate emergency – yet I've enjoyed some of the best fishing on my local river over the last few years.

One particular stretch, which I'd previously ignored because of the lengthy walk required to get there, is now *full* of fish. I only gave it a proper try a couple of years ago, thanks to my minimalist approach, but it quickly rewarded me with numerous double-figure catches featuring scale-perfect roach, dace, chub, bream and perch. I'm one of only a few anglers to fish there and, although it's only a modest cast to the far bank, the water is deep and flows steadily, taking me back to my boyhood visits to Burton Joyce, Gunthorpe Bridge and Newark.

Just like those distant days on the mighty Trent, the best part about this stretch of the Wey is not knowing what the next cast might bring. After a string of small roach, gudgeon or perch, it's always a rush when the quivertip slams over and I feel something much bigger kicking in the depths. And that happened a few times during a particularly memorable session last July when, just as the heat was starting to wane and the walkers and cyclists were thinning out, I was visited by Rachel and some of the kids.

I'd already caught a netful, including some roach up to a pound, a chub of over four pounds and even a small pike that had grabbed a roach on the way in and then managed to get hooked itself, so I was happy to let them have a go. Bites were almost guaranteed and they all managed to hit at least one of them – thereby enjoying a novel interlude to their evening stroll and gaining some appreciation that fishing isn't all about sitting still and waiting.

During other recent visits, I've been drawn to nostalgic methods, baits and species of fish, like trotting a stick float with hemp and tares for roach, or ledgering bread-flake for chub in the winter. Variety being the spice of life, this kind of experimentation is something else I encourage any jaded or time-poor people to try. Indeed, judging by the angling press, remaining tackle shop shelves and YouTube, carp fishing no longer has quite the same, vice-like grip on young people entering the sport.

While big carp understandably remain one of the most coveted of freshwater fish, there seems to be growing interest in other coarse species like perch, tench, barbel and crucians. Even commercial fisheries are increasingly being developed where 'silvers' take pride of place, while there has also been a resurgence in big matches being held on natural venues, which is all encouraging I think.

Again, I have no problem spending a day at a well-managed commercial – and I enjoy trying to catch a ton or more of carp as much as the next match angler – but, for me, the thrills are strongest while exploring less manicured or predictable waters. It's one of the oldest sayings in the game, but fishing really *is* about more than catching fish. It's always nice to be successful, but being on the bank can also be about tranquillity, fresh air, marvelling at wildlife or socialising with friends and family.

Now recognised as a fantastic remedy for mental health issues, ranging from anxiety to depression, angling can involve long walks and gentle exercise, or simply sitting under the shade of a tree and utterly losing oneself in the landscape. And if the aim of hiking might be to explore new areas of countryside or enjoy moving through a range of scenery, both of which I enjoy doing, fishing is often about immersion in one place. Always with the enchanting element of water.

Whether catching fish or not, over time, it's possible to become completely absorbed and feel genuinely in tune with one's surroundings. Even small changes in the weather are tangible, unlike the sterile view through a double-glazed window, while reflections, scents and wildlife can become intimately familiar.

Some might argue it's possible to experience the same, trance-like state merely by sitting near a lake or stream. And I wouldn't knock anyone for doing just that, but I maintain that trying to guess what's happening beneath the surface and using hard-won skills and experience, or indeed a bit of luck, to connect with something hidden and unpredictable, adds an extra and truly deeper dimension.

During these troubling times of climate change, COVID-19, racial injustice and many other societal inequalities, I think nature is more vital than ever to us humans – clearly in terms of our survival being dependent on stopping the damage we keep doing to the planet, but also its astounding power to heal our bodies and minds.

If you've lost or don't recognise this connection, or feel in need of a little relaxation and inspiration, I urge you to enjoy the natural world however and whenever you can. It doesn't matter if that means sitting on a park bench, walking along a cliff-top, planting seeds in a pot or escaping on a camping trip – you will benefit in some small way. For me, however, there's nothing quite so magical as fishing and if you understand that too, or want to give it a try, then get out there soon.

Acknowledgements

If you have read my preface, which was originally typed some four or five years before I finally finished *The Magic of Fishing*, you will know that having it published is a dream come true. The knowledge that a collection of highly personal, very special memories may be read and enjoyed by others – no matter how few – has brought me immeasurable joy, pride and satisfaction. And it may never have happened if it weren't for the encouragement of Rachel, my wife, plus my magical parents and a handful of fishing friends who were in the know throughout the tortuous process – including Andy Aukland and Jim Baxter.

Even then, I faced challenges and further delays, because writing a book is one thing, yet finding a publisher is entirely another. I initially approached all the traditional angling specialists, who were good enough to read my sample chapters and provide positive feedback but, ultimately, they all felt it wasn't "commercial enough" because I'm not a well-known name. This consistent stance seemed fair enough and I was convinced I would need to self-publish – until one day when Joe, my youngest brother, came to the rescue.

As a Sheffield-based firefighter he is used to rescuing people, but he's also had a number of works published, all of them by Great Northern Books. And during the first national lockdown, in the spring of 2020, he decided it couldn't hurt to introduce me to the marvellous David Burrill. I dropped him a line and we bonded almost instantly over email. So, although I am yet to meet him in person, I undoubtedly have his experience, wit, wisdom and open mind to thank for the fact this book now exists in print. It is he and Joe who made the full extent of my dream become reality and I will be forever grateful to them both. David, Granddad would have liked your gambling spirit.

I should commit to a 'last cast' soon, but I must also thank my brilliant dad for his patience and magical pencil sketches, plus Anna, my talented artist sister, who designed the stunning cover for *The Magic of Fishing*. Indeed, gratitude is due to all of my family who have read the draft book, given me encouragement and may even buy a copy with their own hard-earned money.

Finally, thanks to Amanda Picken, my fishermuggle-yet-professional proof-reader, and to all my generous test readers. They include Jim, Andy, Steve, Ben; plus several members of DWSSC, including Dennis, John and Mick; the genial Bill Rushmer, formerly a prolific feature writer with *The Angler's Mail*; Dom Garnett of *Angling Times* fame, who kindly provided the wonderful foreword; and David Aylward, head bailiff of Byfleet AA, an accomplished fisherman and collector of fishing books, who not only liked the manuscript but is still trying to help me catch a big barbel.